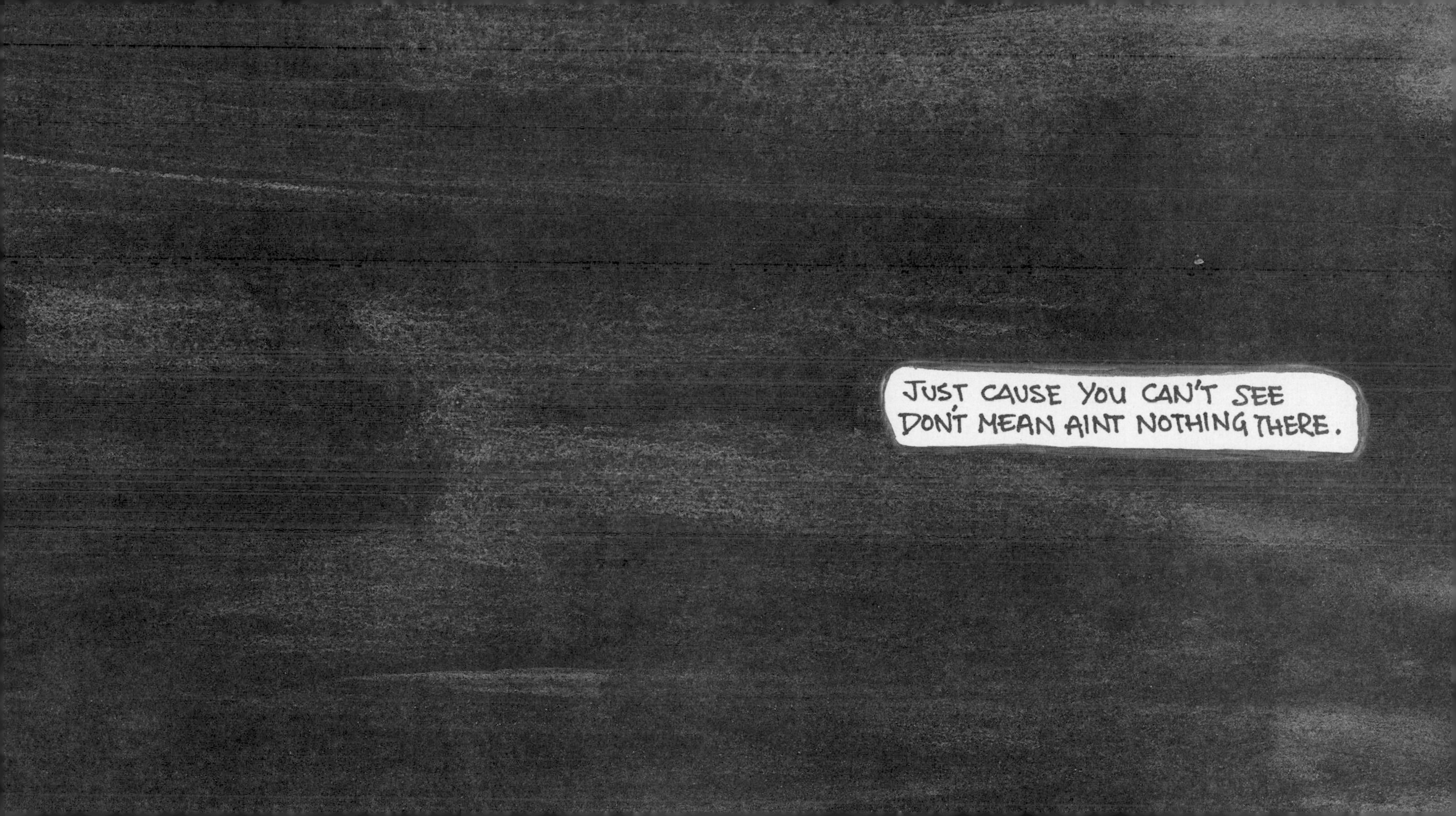
JUST CAUSE YOU CAN'T SEE DON'T MEAN AINT NOTHING THERE.

PITCH BLACK

DON'T BE SKERD

YOUME
and
ANTHONY HORTON

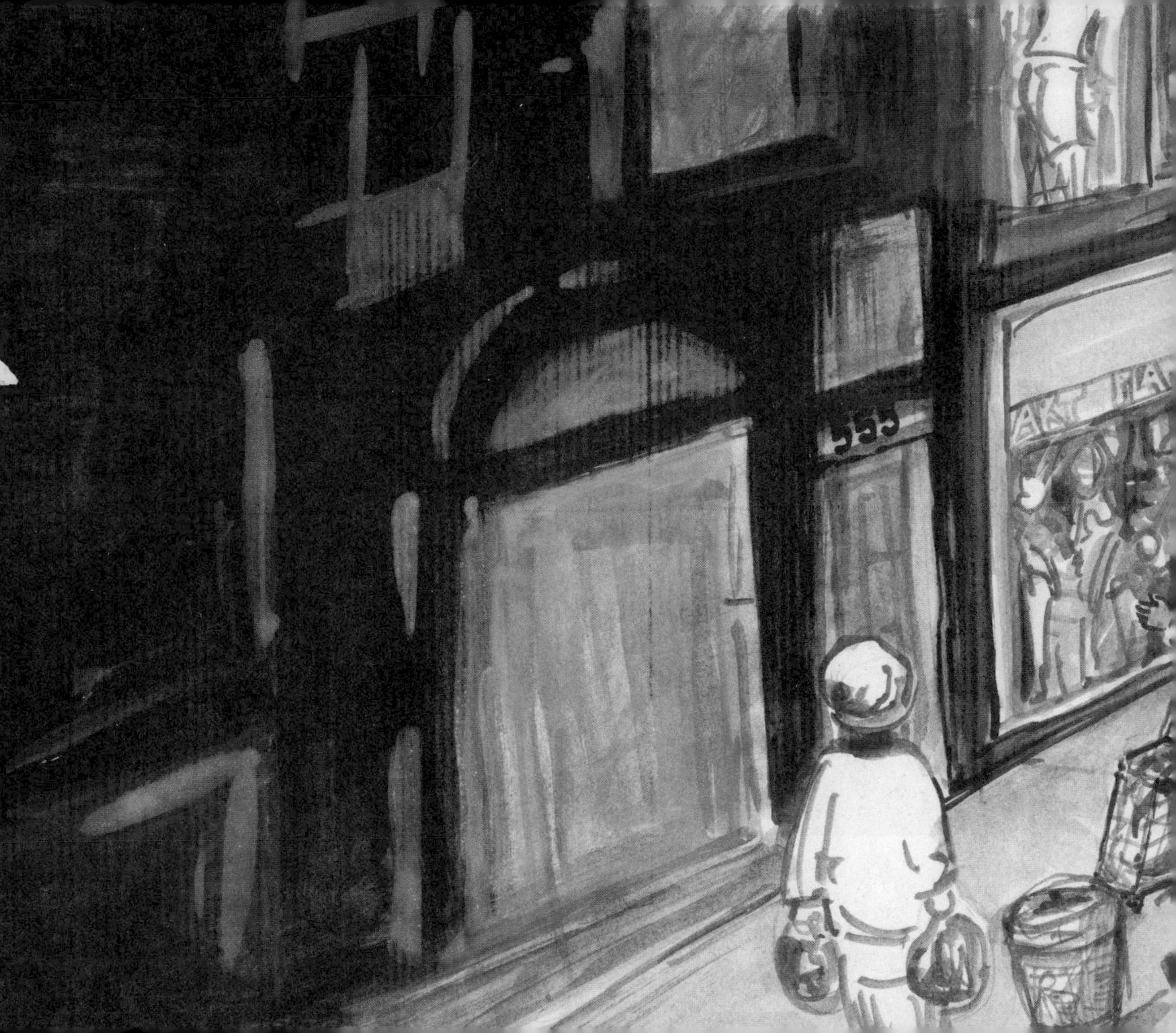
555

CINCO PUNTOS PRESS
AN IMPRINT OF LEE & LOW BOOKS INC.
NEW YORK

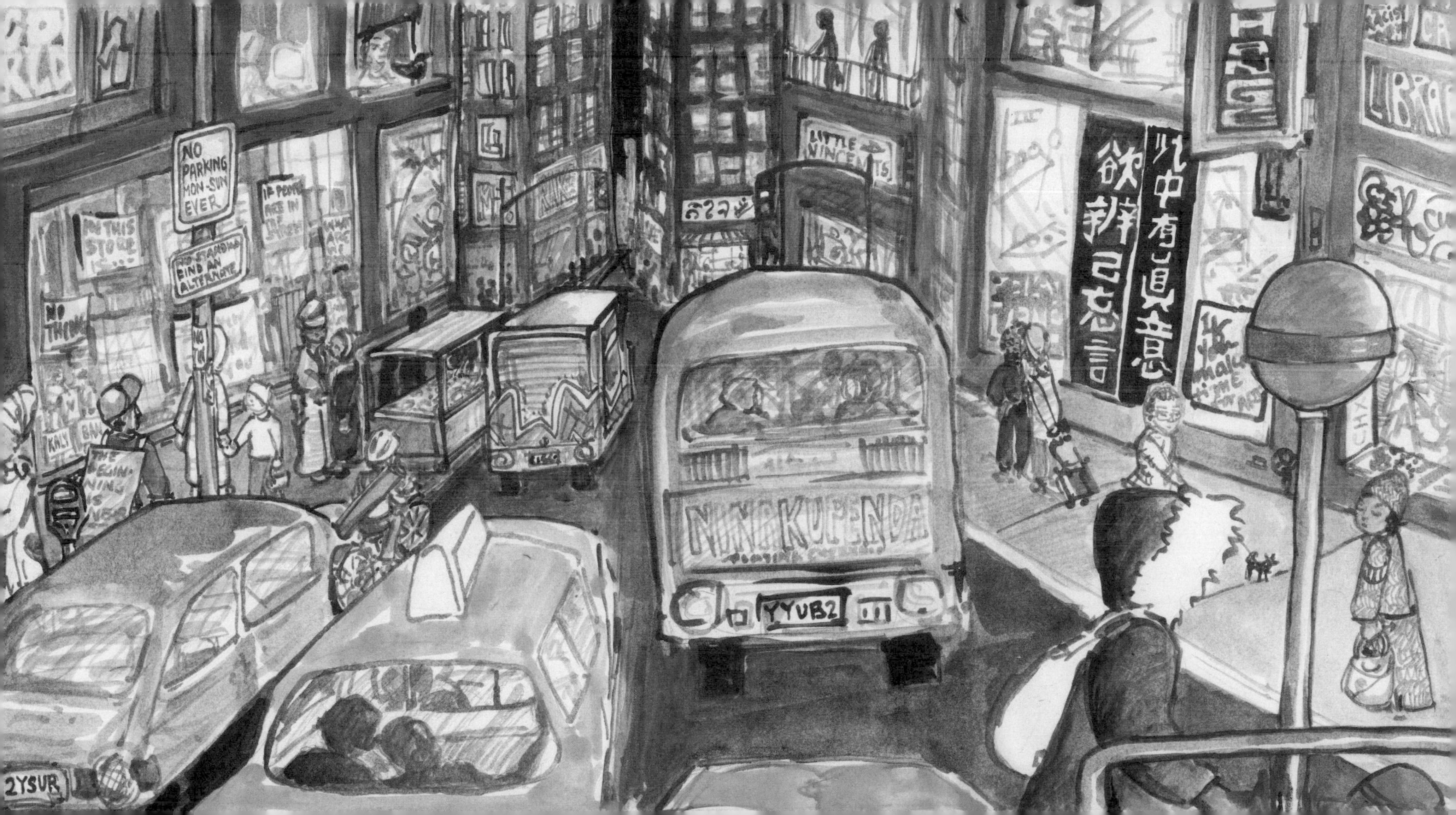
NO PARKING MON-SUN EVER
LITTLE VINCENTS
此中有真意
欲辨已忘言
NINAKUPENDA
YYUB2
2YSUR

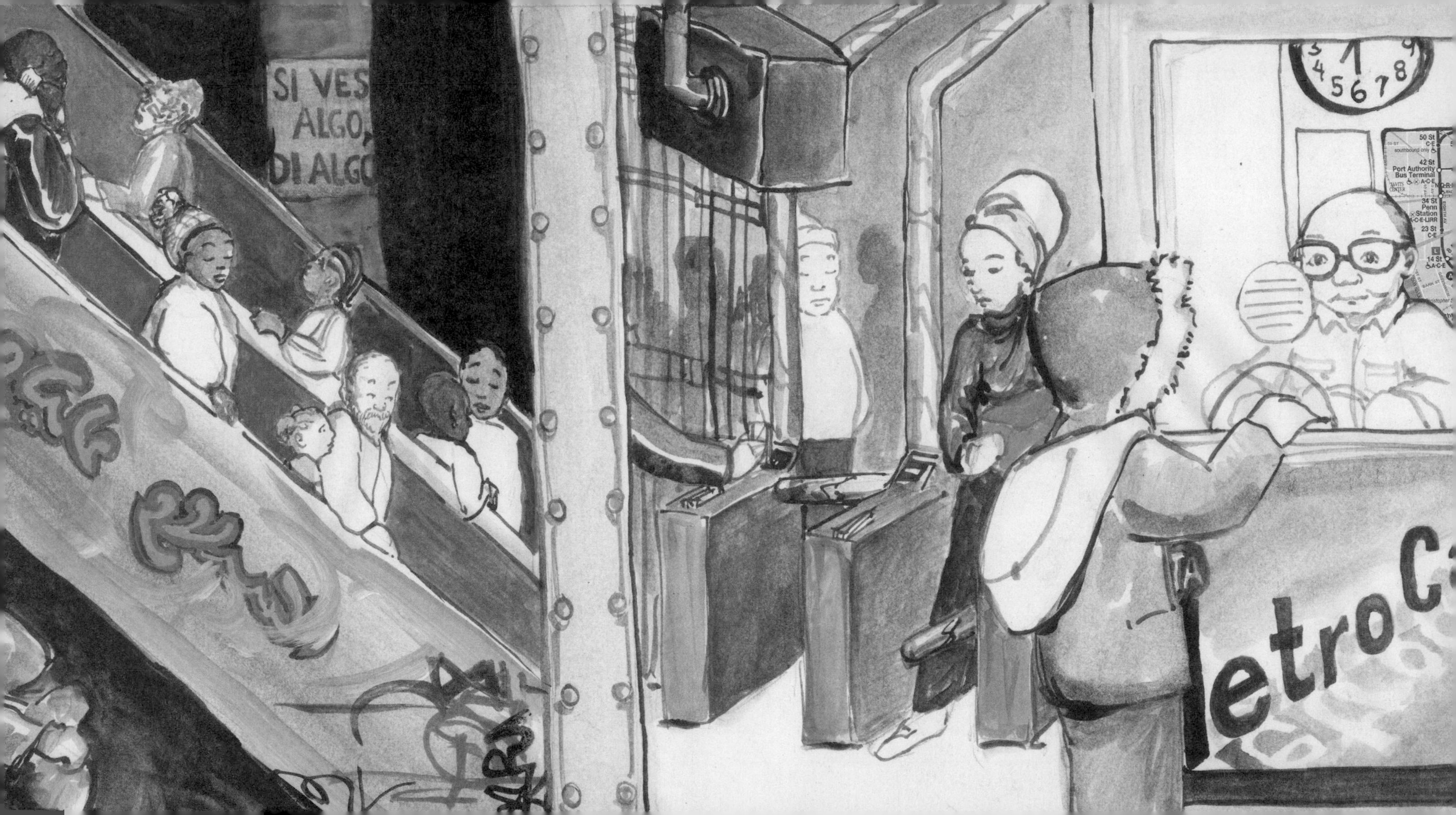
SI VES
ALGO,
DI ALGO

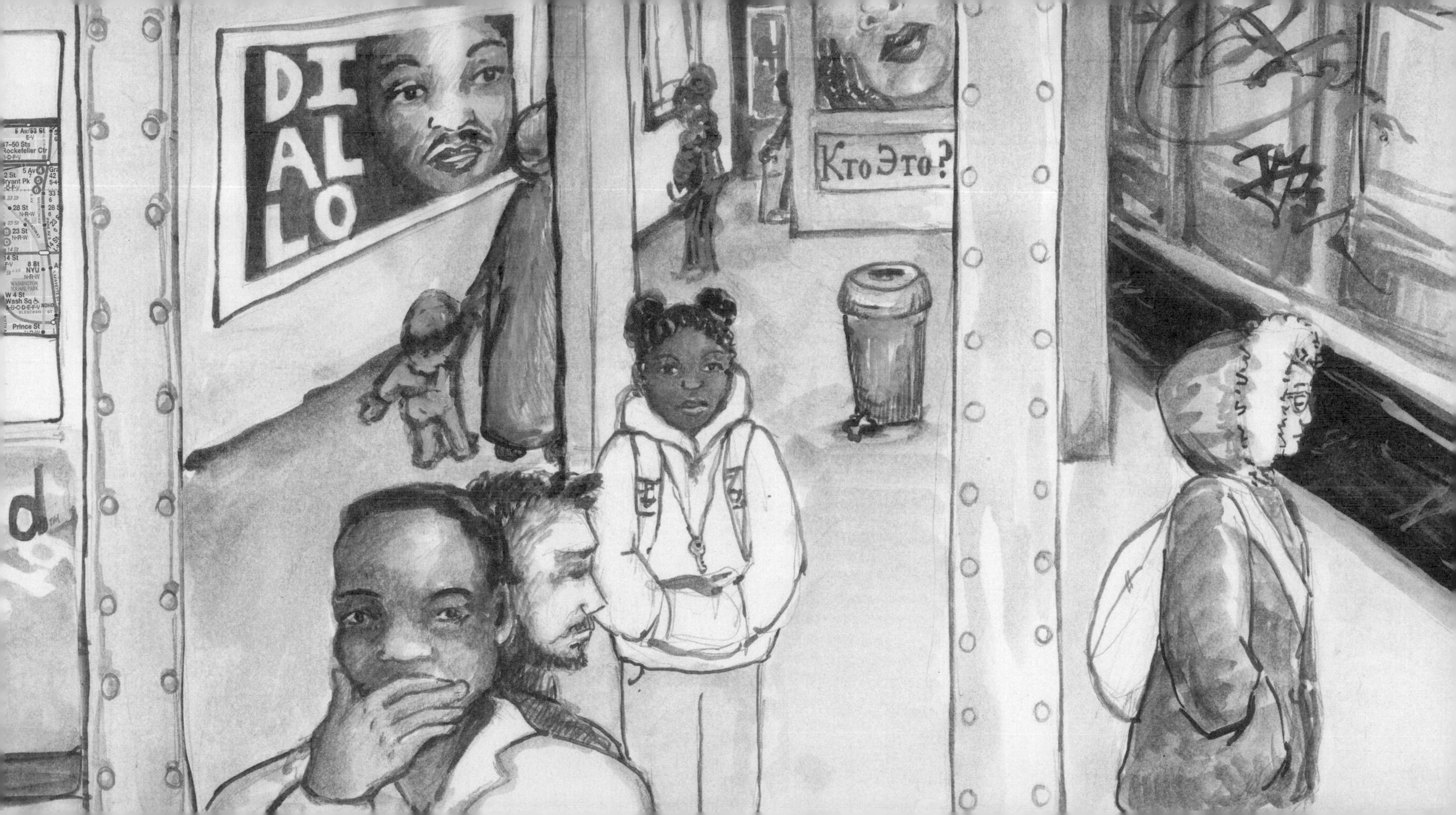
DI
AL
LO
Кто Это?

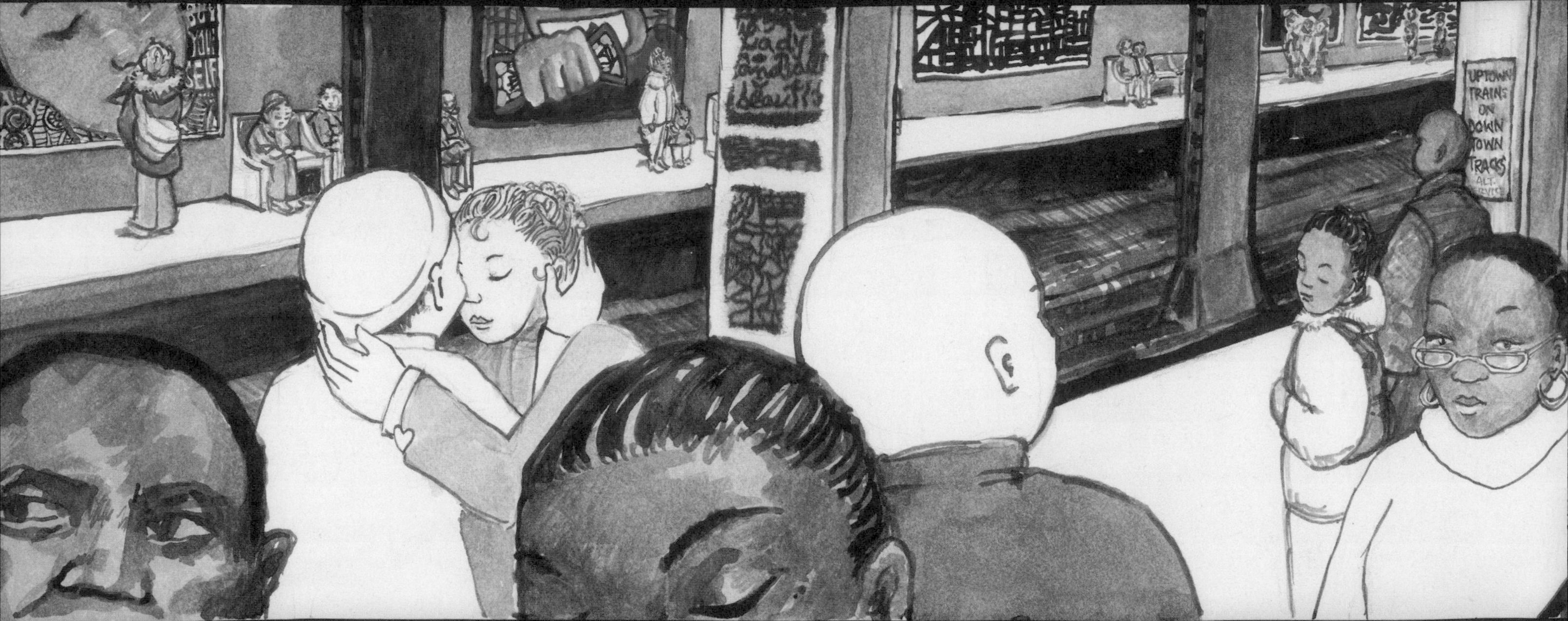
UPTOWN TRAINS ON DOWNTOWN TRACKS
ALT.

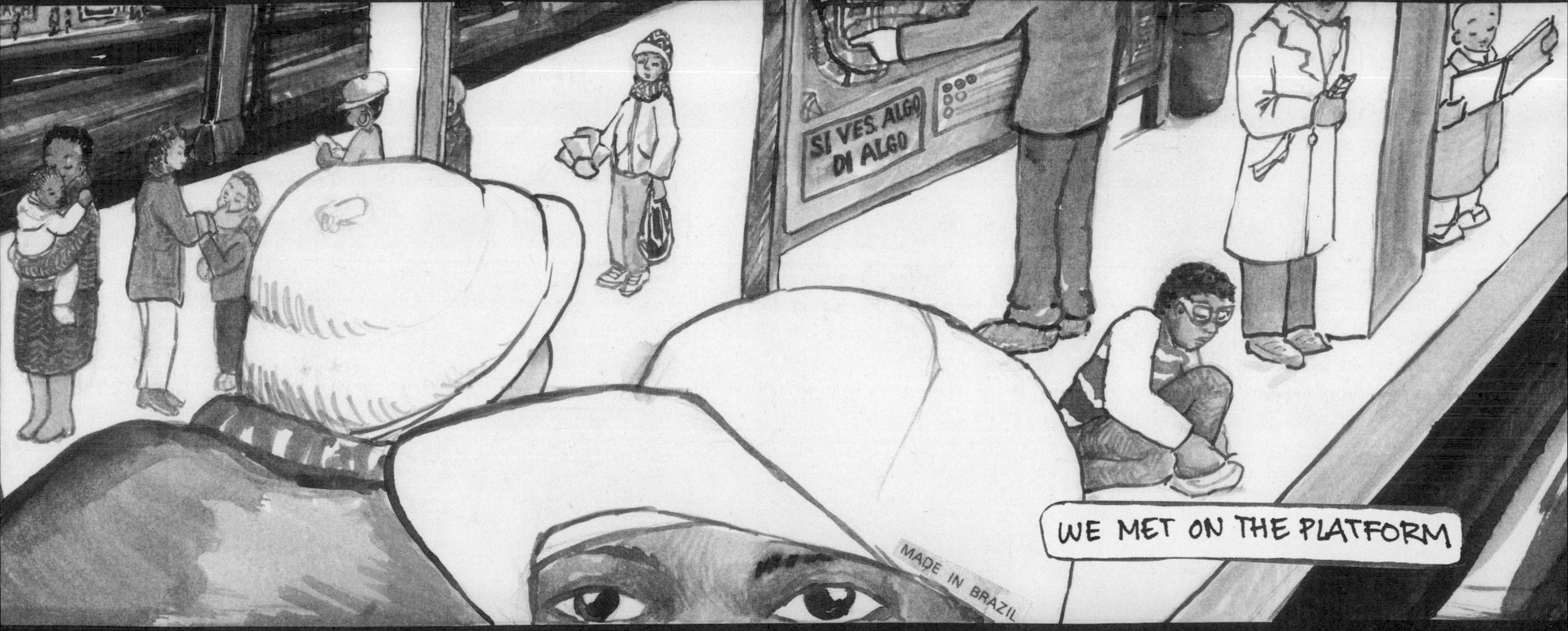
SI VES ALGO
DI ALGO
MADE IN BRAZIL
WE MET ON THE PLATFORM

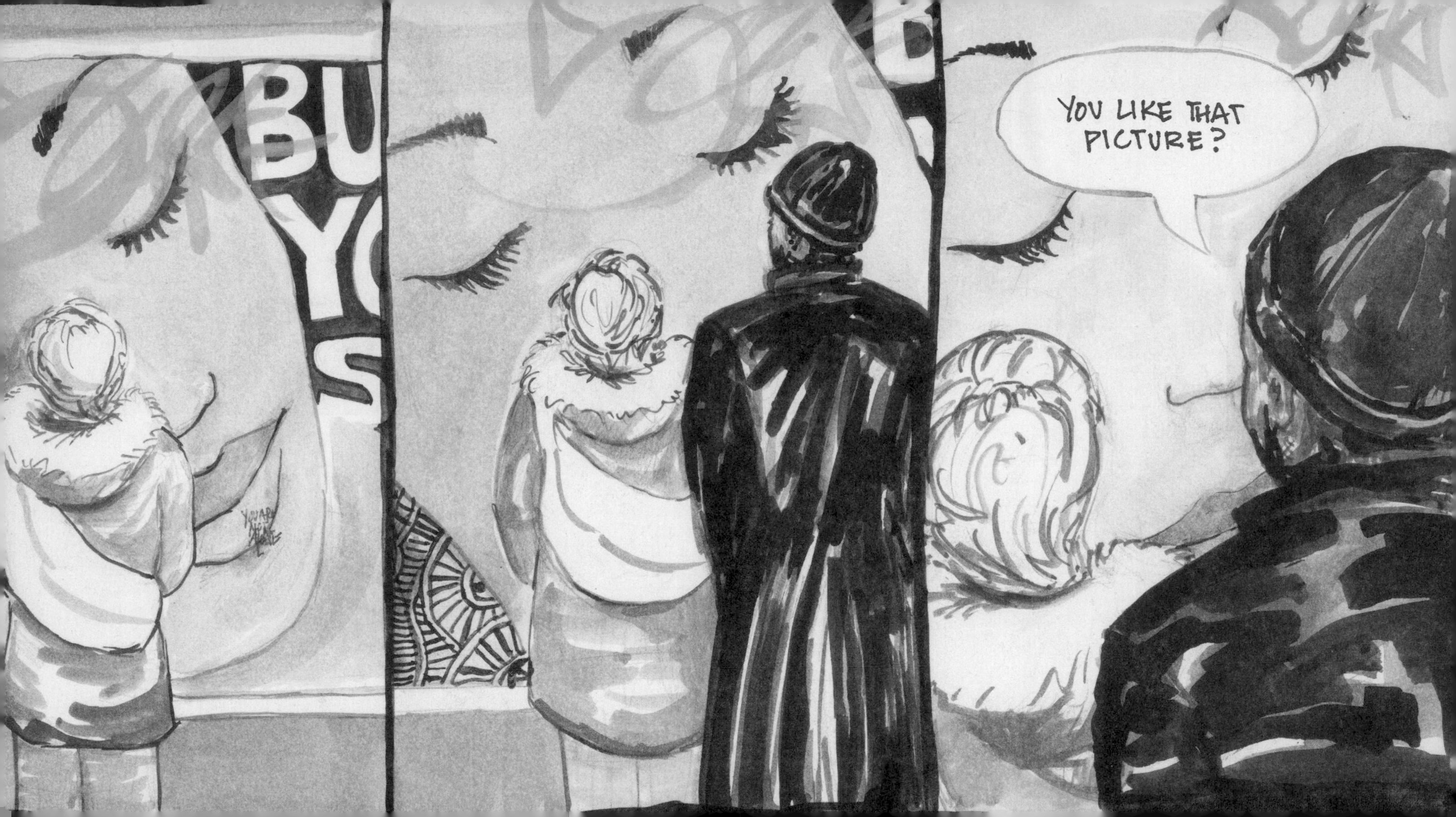
YOU LIKE THAT PICTURE?

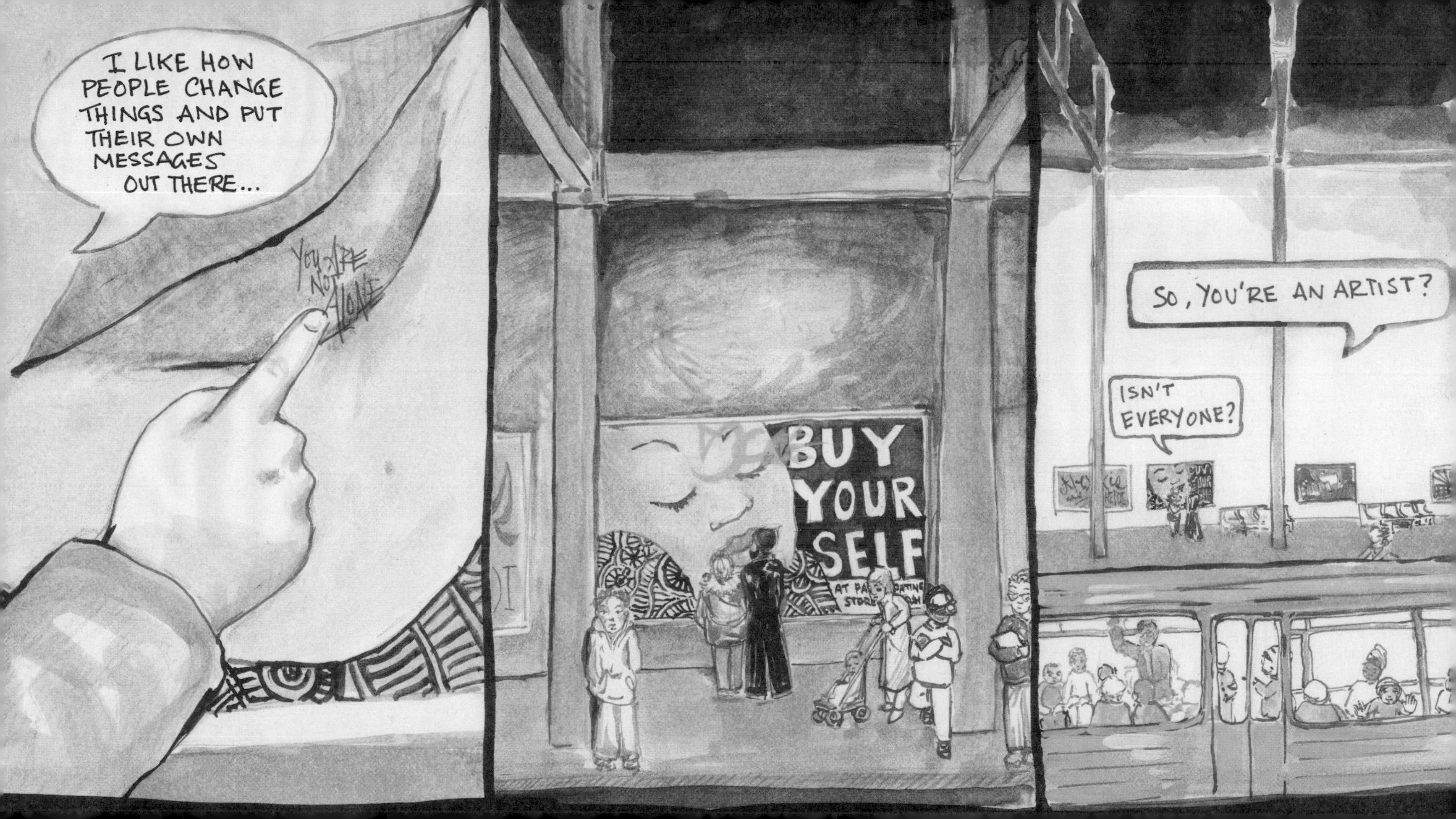
I LIKE HOW PEOPLE CHANGE THINGS AND PUT THEIR OWN MESSAGES OUT THERE...
YOU ARE NOT ALONE
BUY YOUR SELF
SO, YOU'RE AN ARTIST?
ISN'T EVERYONE?

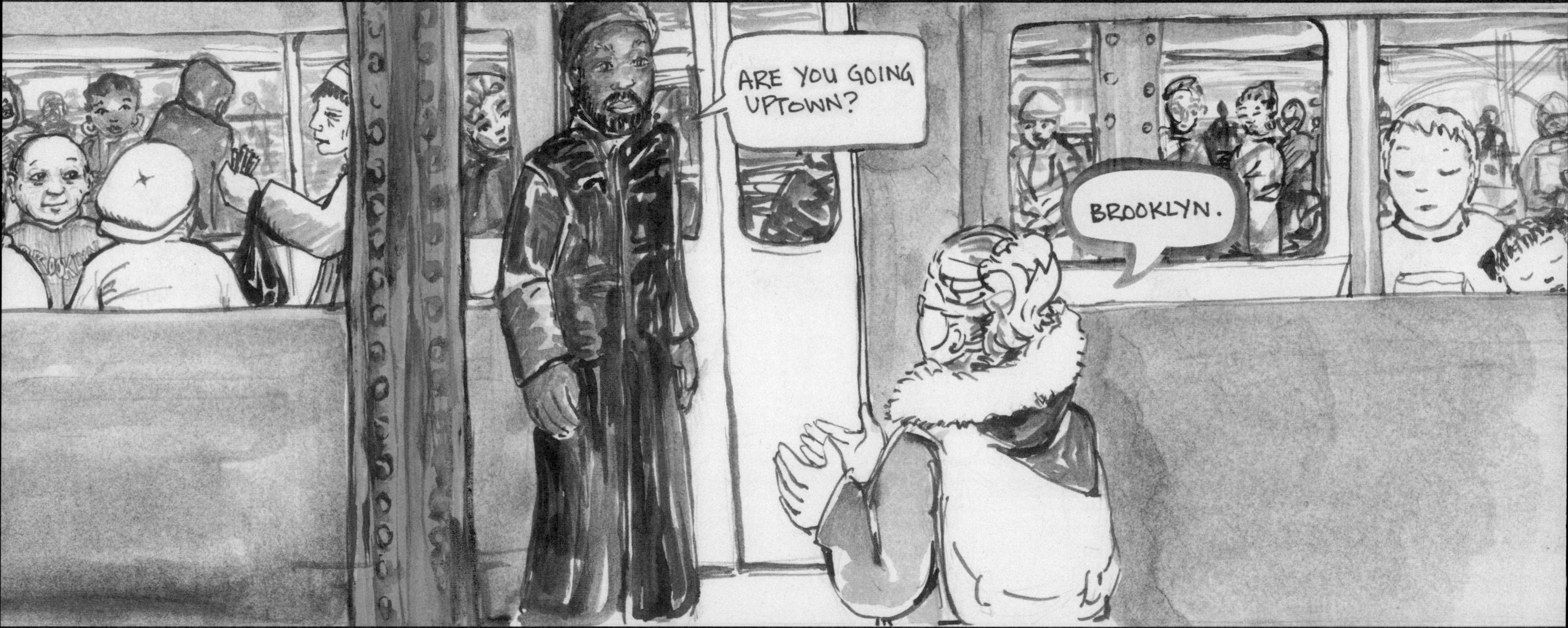
ARE YOU GOING UPTOWN?
BROOKLYN.

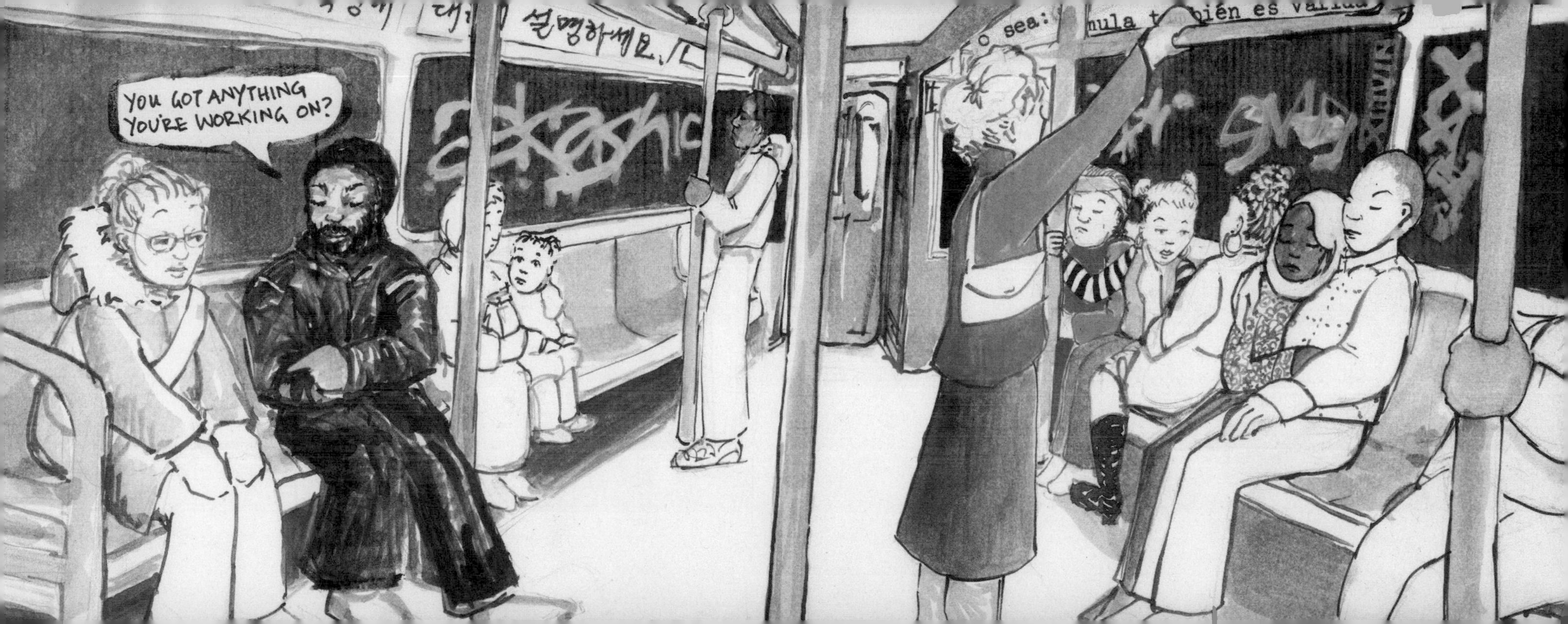
YOU GOT ANYTHING YOU'RE WORKING ON?

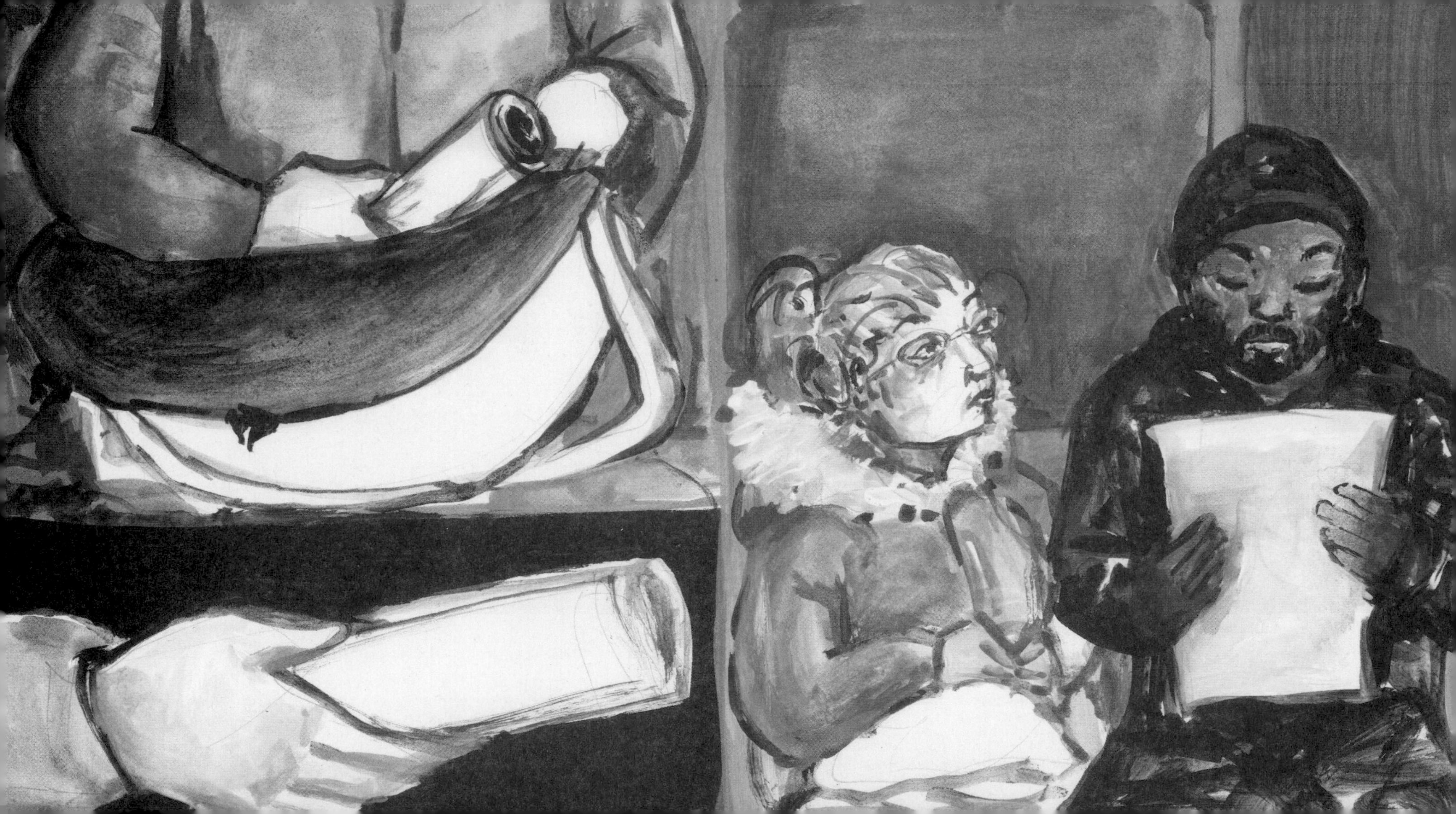

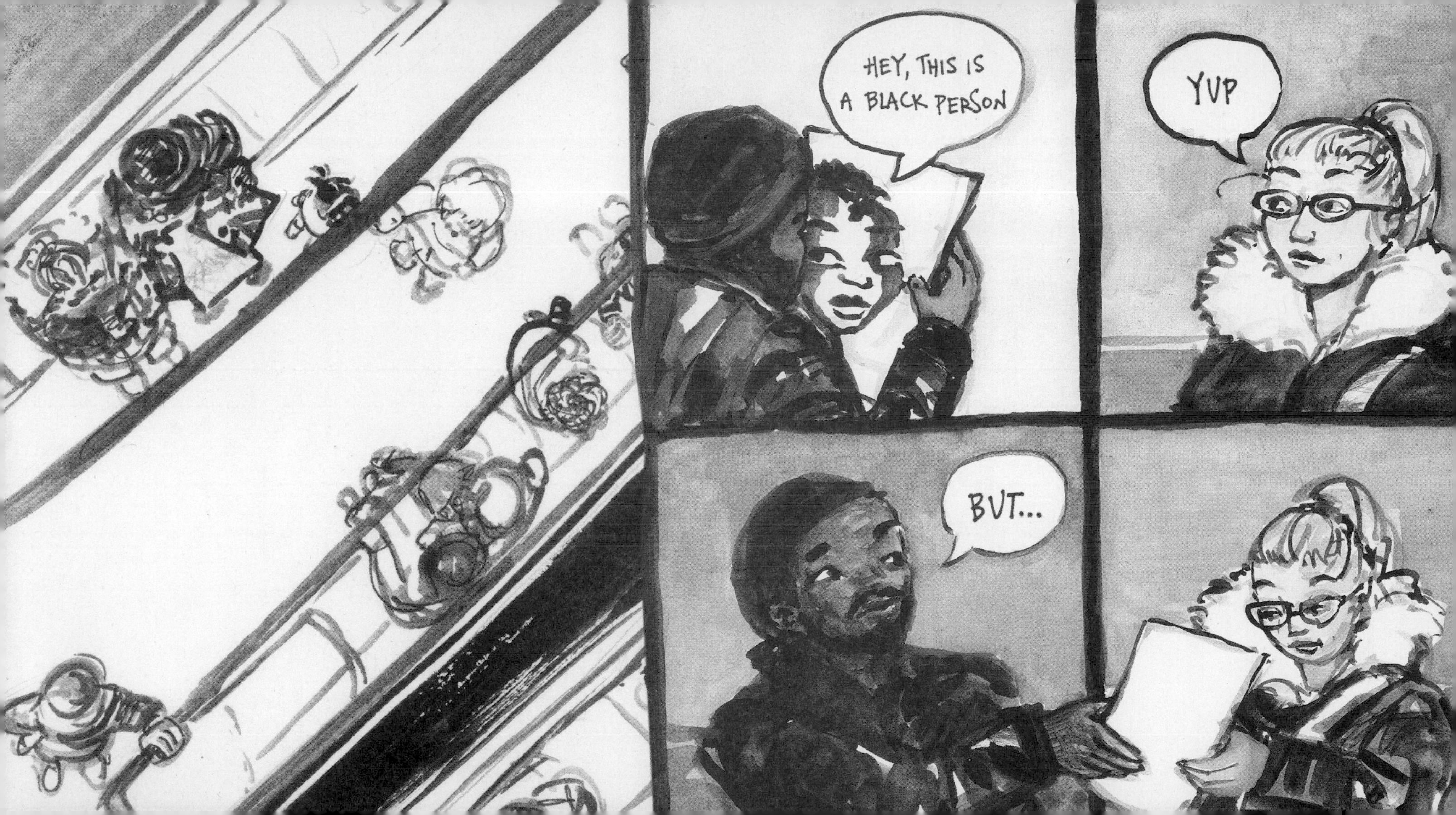
HEY, THIS IS A BLACK PERSON
YUP
BUT...

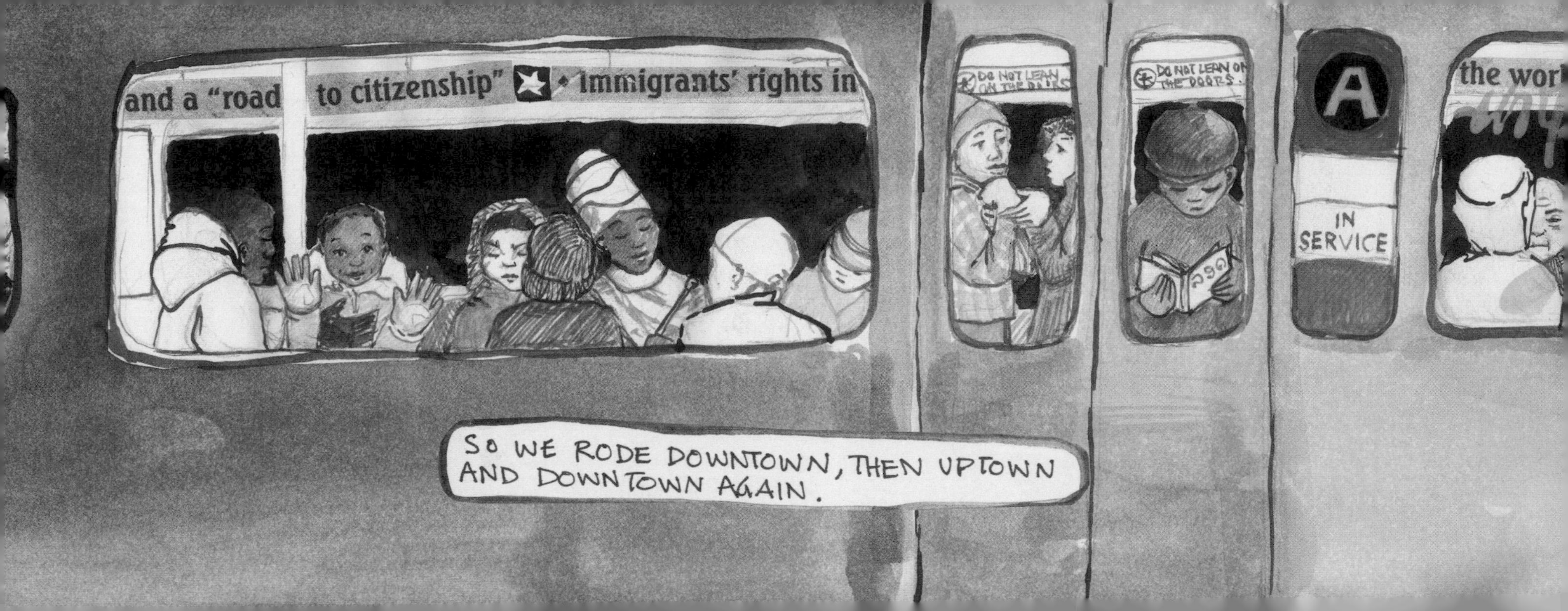
and a "road to citizenship" ✦ immigrants' rights in
DO NOT LEAN ON THE DOORS
A
IN SERVICE
the wor
SO WE RODE DOWNTOWN, THEN UPTOWN AND DOWNTOWN AGAIN.

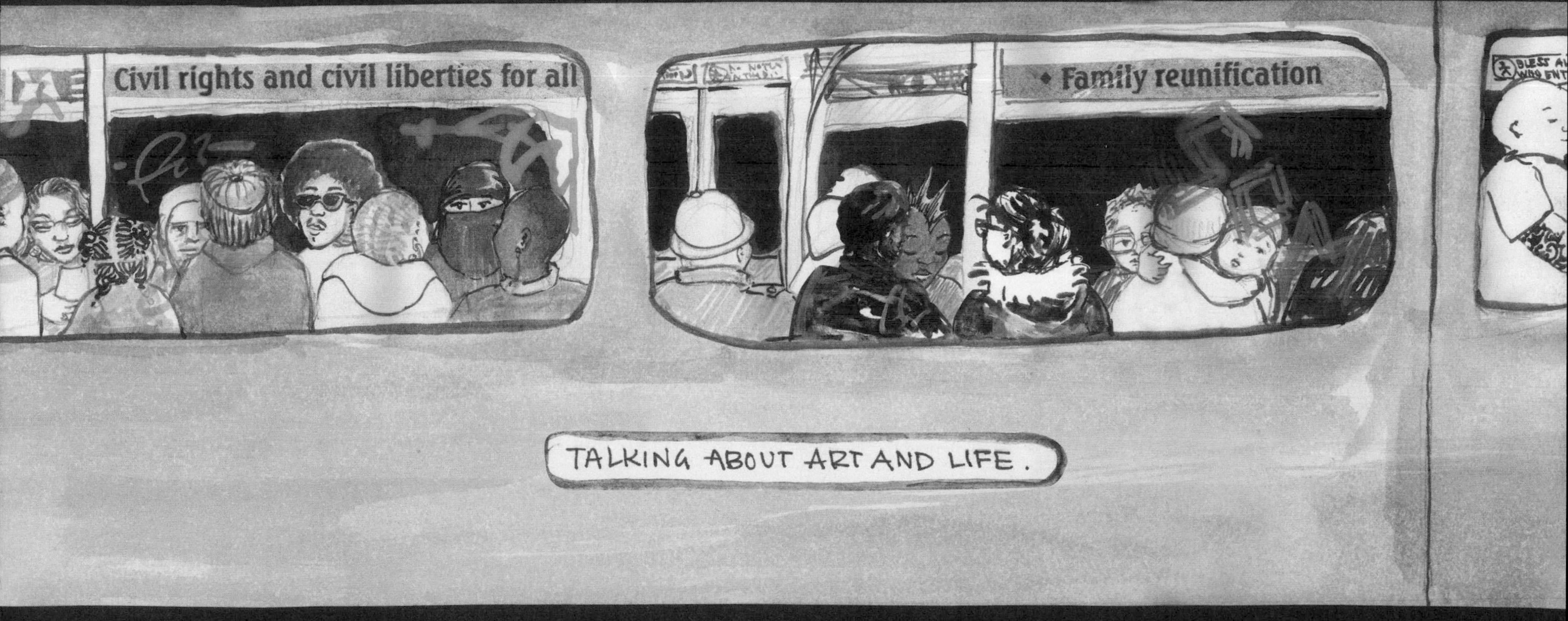
Civil rights and civil liberties for all
Family reunification
TALKING ABOUT ART AND LIFE.

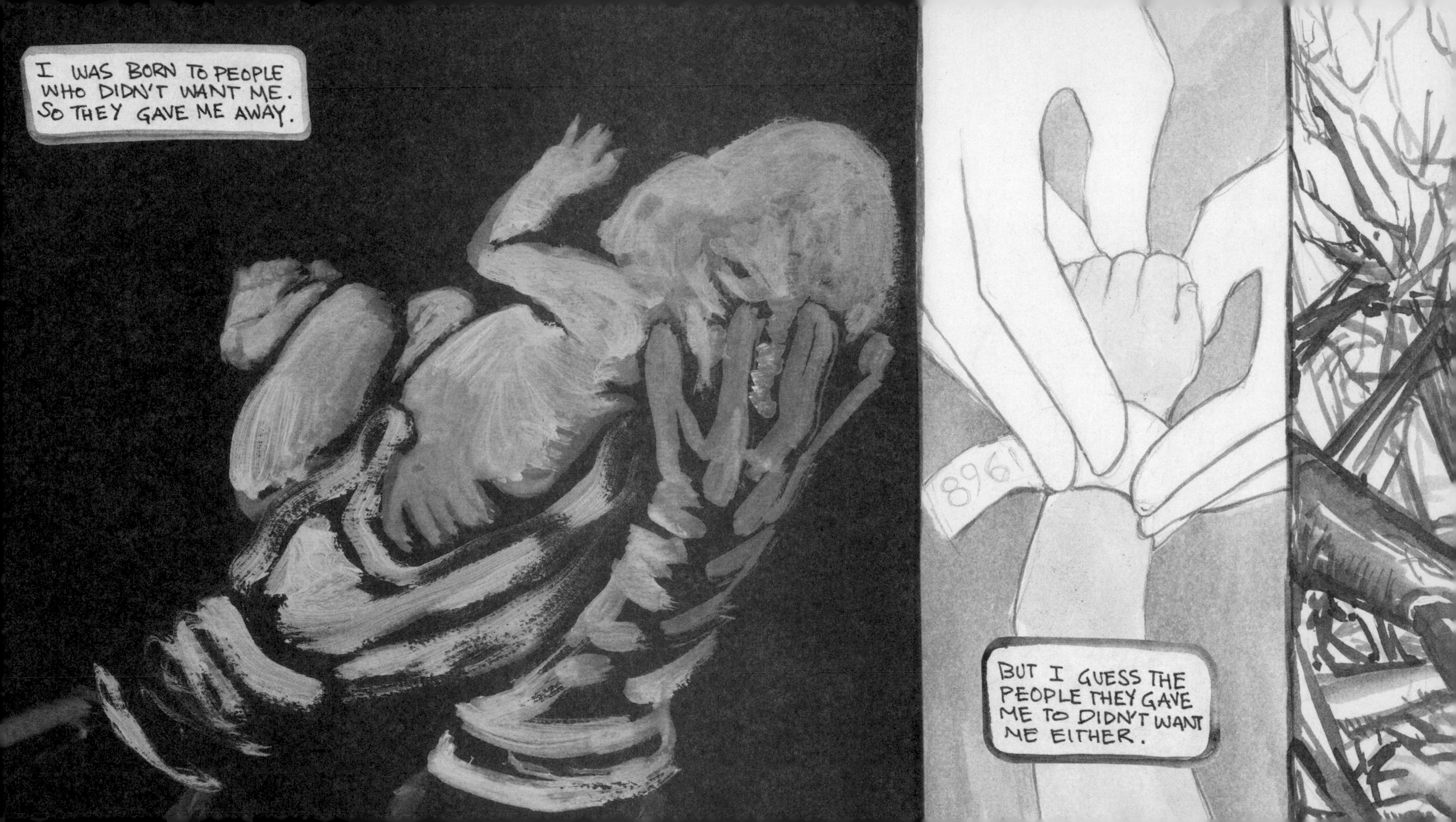
I WAS BORN TO PEOPLE WHO DIDN'T WANT ME. SO THEY GAVE ME AWAY.
1968
BUT I GUESS THE PEOPLE THEY GAVE ME TO DIDN'T WANT ME EITHER.

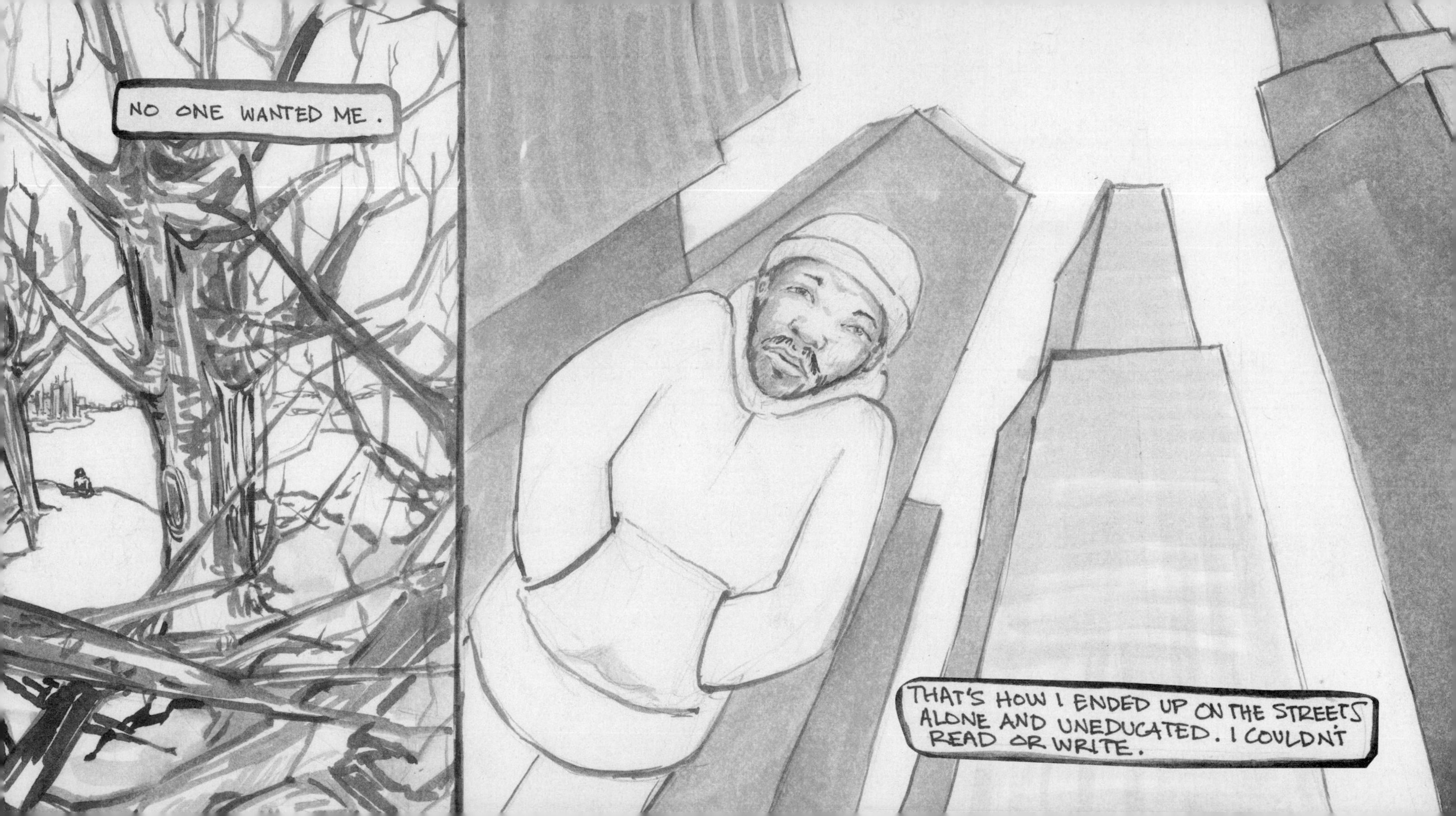
NO ONE WANTED ME.
THAT'S HOW I ENDED UP ON THE STREETS ALONE AND UNEDUCATED. I COULDN'T READ OR WRITE.

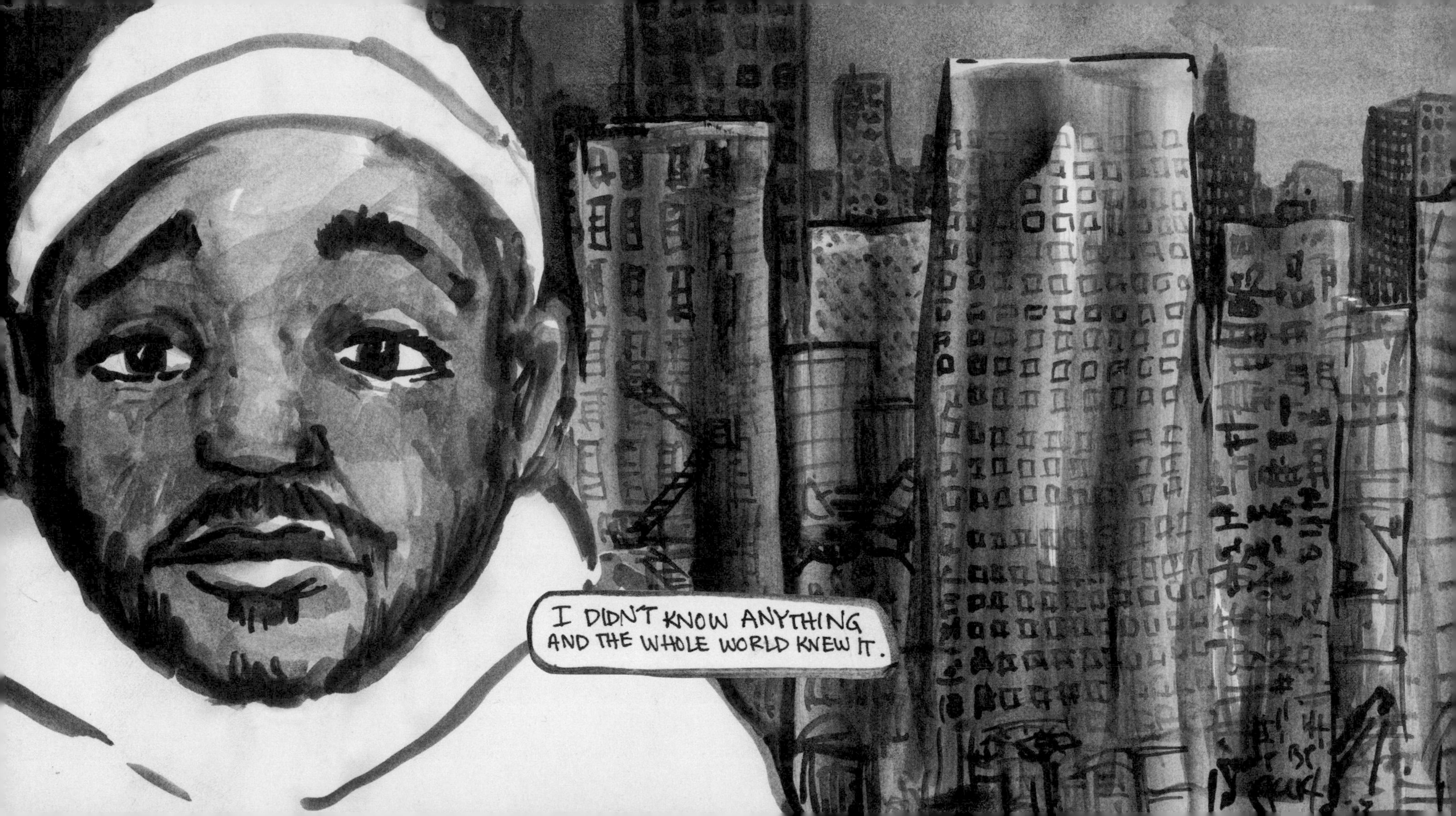
I DIDN'T KNOW ANYTHING AND THE WHOLE WORLD KNEW IT.

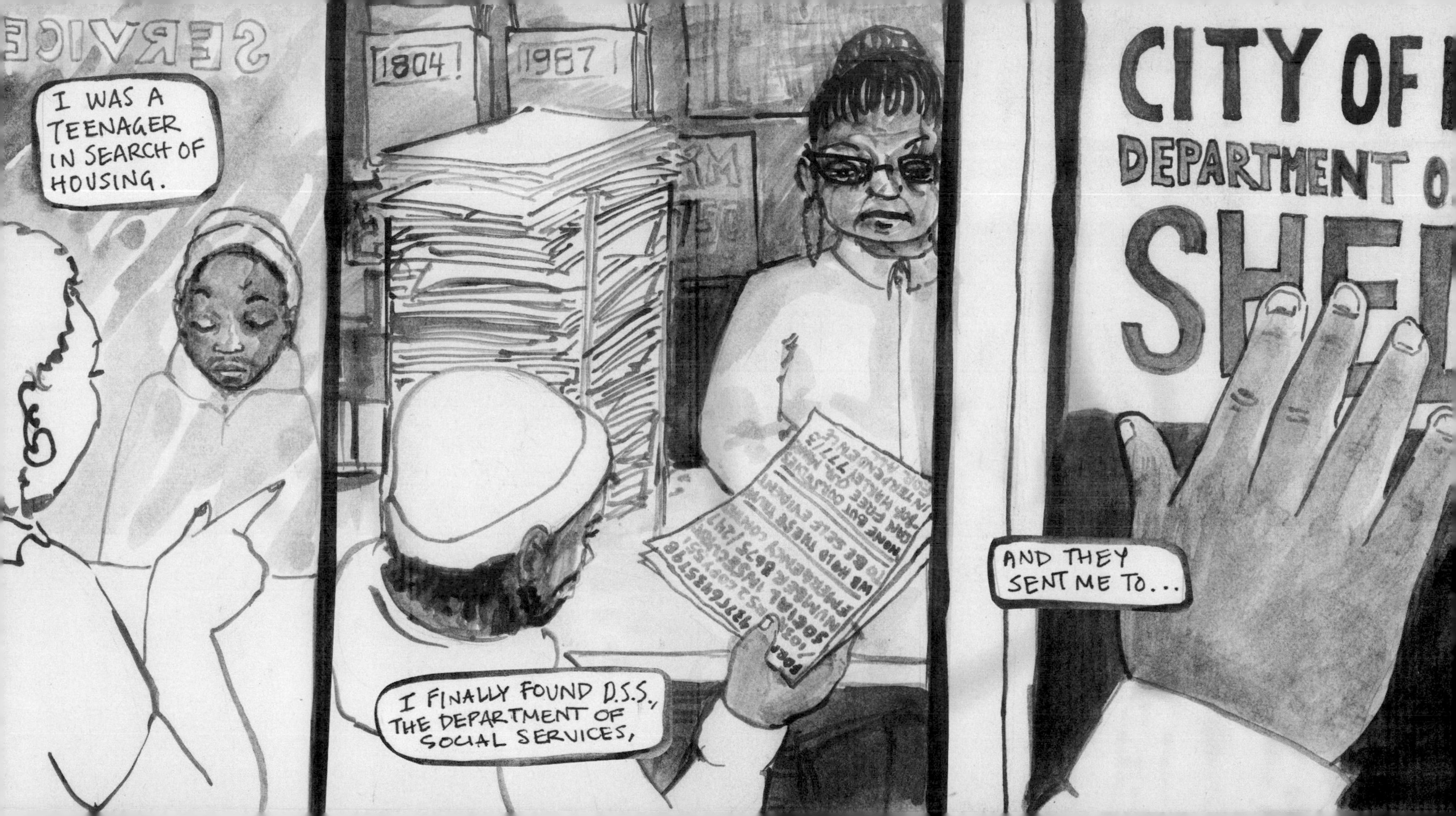
SERVICE
I WAS A TEENAGER IN SEARCH OF HOUSING.
1804
1987
I FINALLY FOUND D.S.S., THE DEPARTMENT OF SOCIAL SERVICES,
CITY OF
DEPARTMENT
AND THEY SENT ME TO...

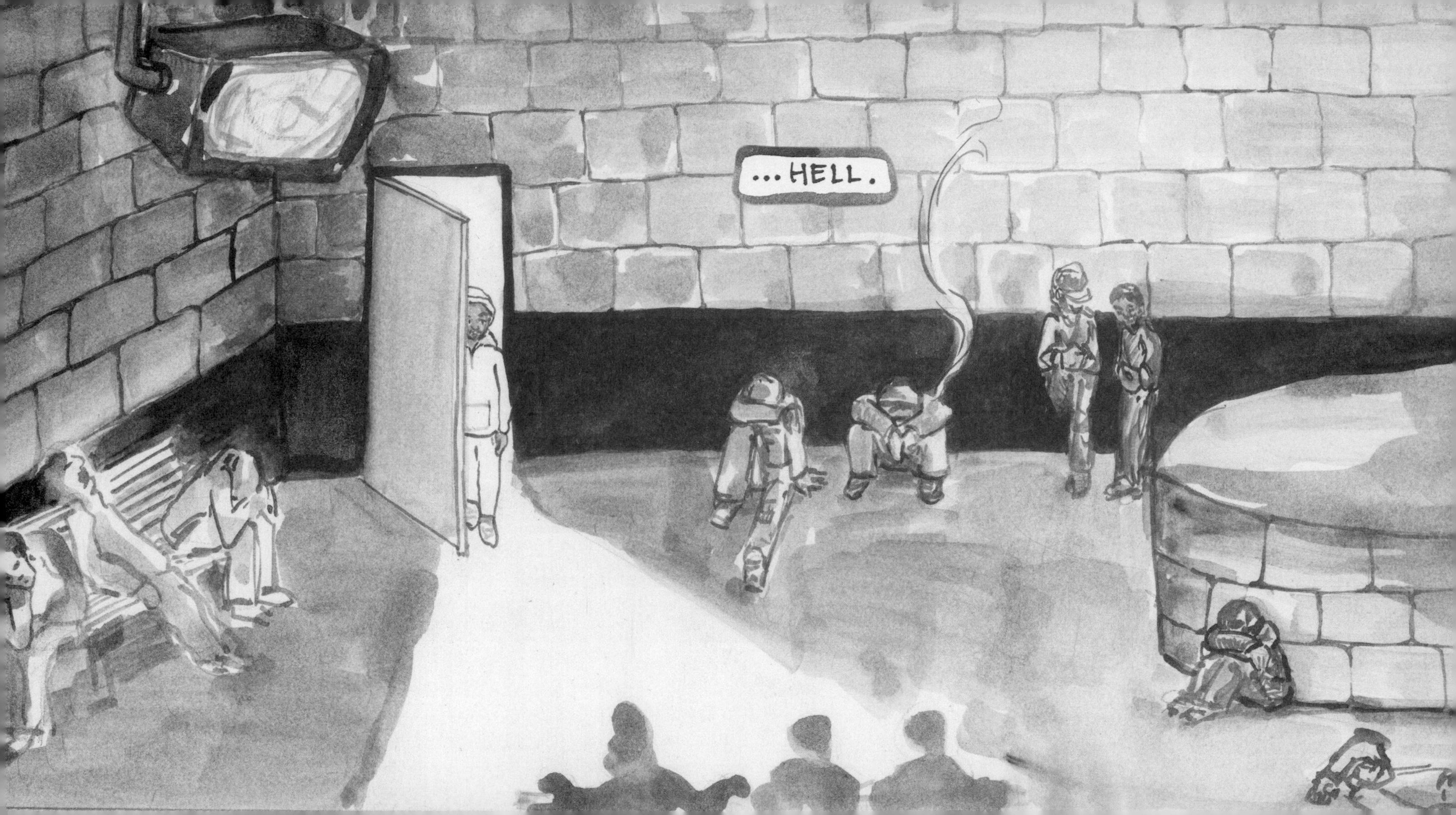
...HELL.

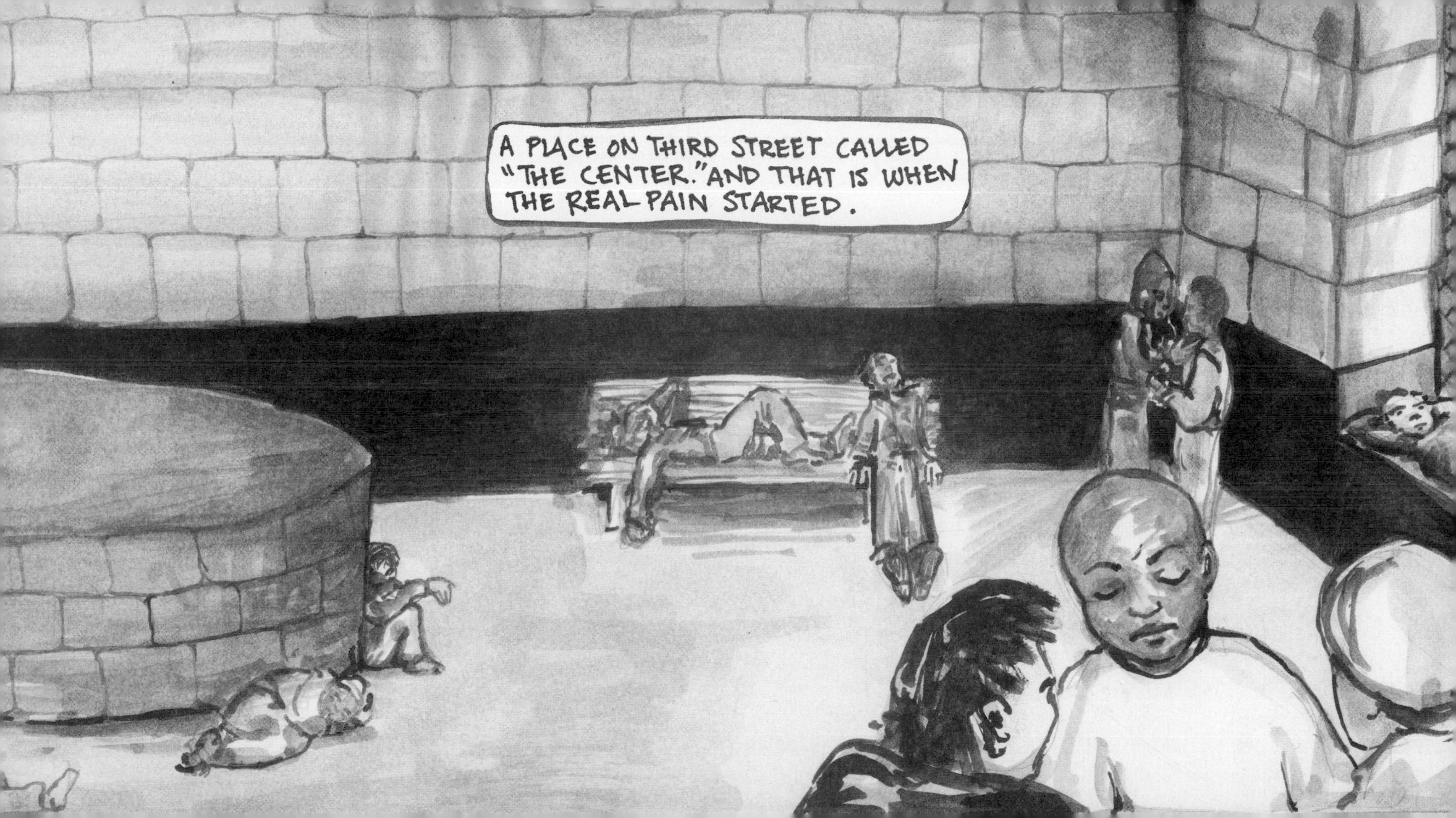
A PLACE ON THIRD STREET CALLED "THE CENTER." AND THAT IS WHEN THE REAL PAIN STARTED.

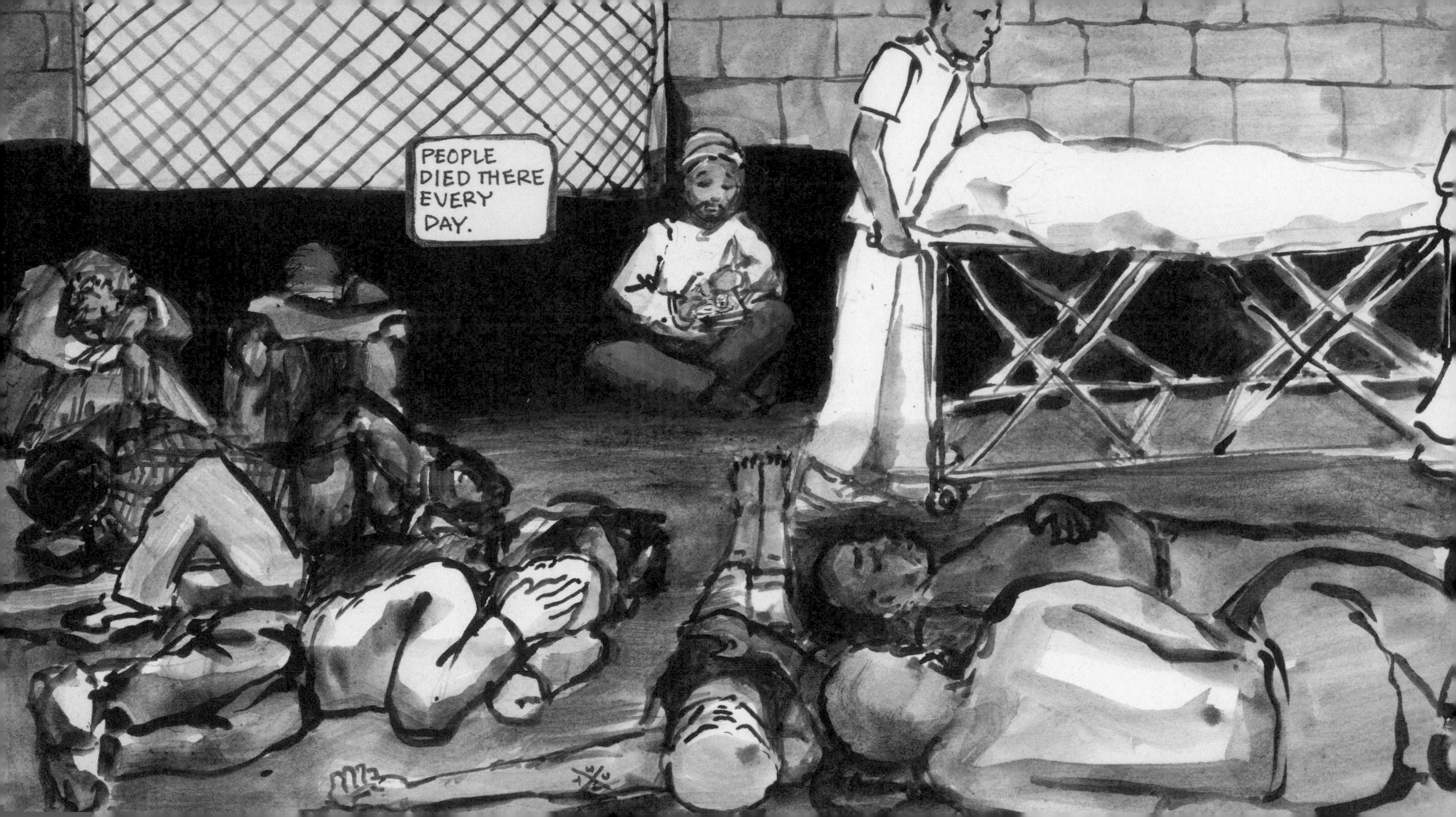
PEOPLE DIED THERE EVERY DAY.

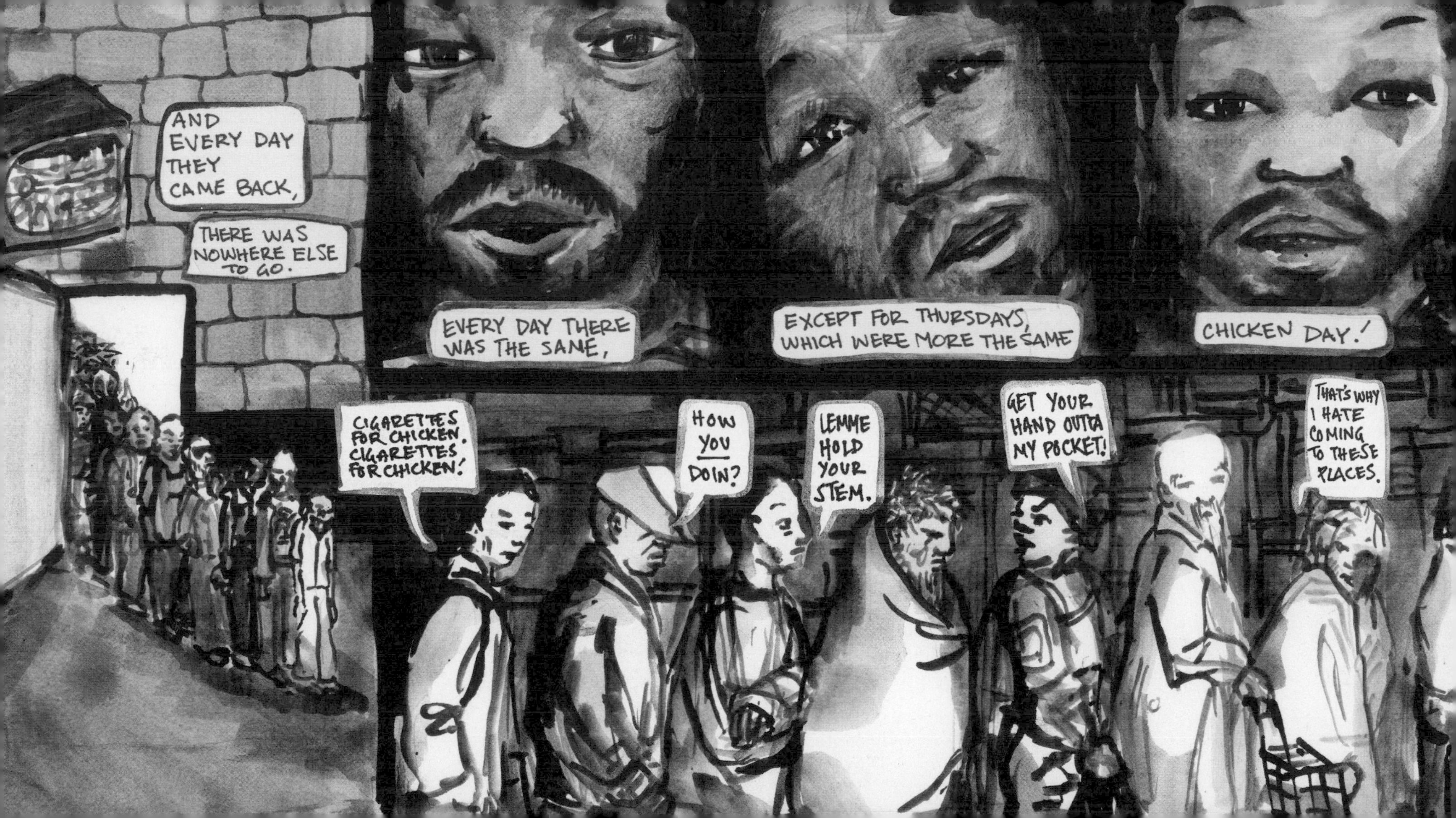
AND EVERY DAY THEY CAME BACK,
THERE WAS NOWHERE ELSE TO GO.
EVERY DAY THERE WAS THE SAME,
EXCEPT FOR THURSDAYS, WHICH WERE MORE THE SAME
CHICKEN DAY!
CIGARETTES FOR CHICKEN. CIGARETTES FOR CHICKEN!
HOW YOU DOIN?
LEMME HOLD YOUR STEM.
GET YOUR HAND OUTTA MY POCKET!
THAT'S WHY I HATE COMING TO THESE PLACES.

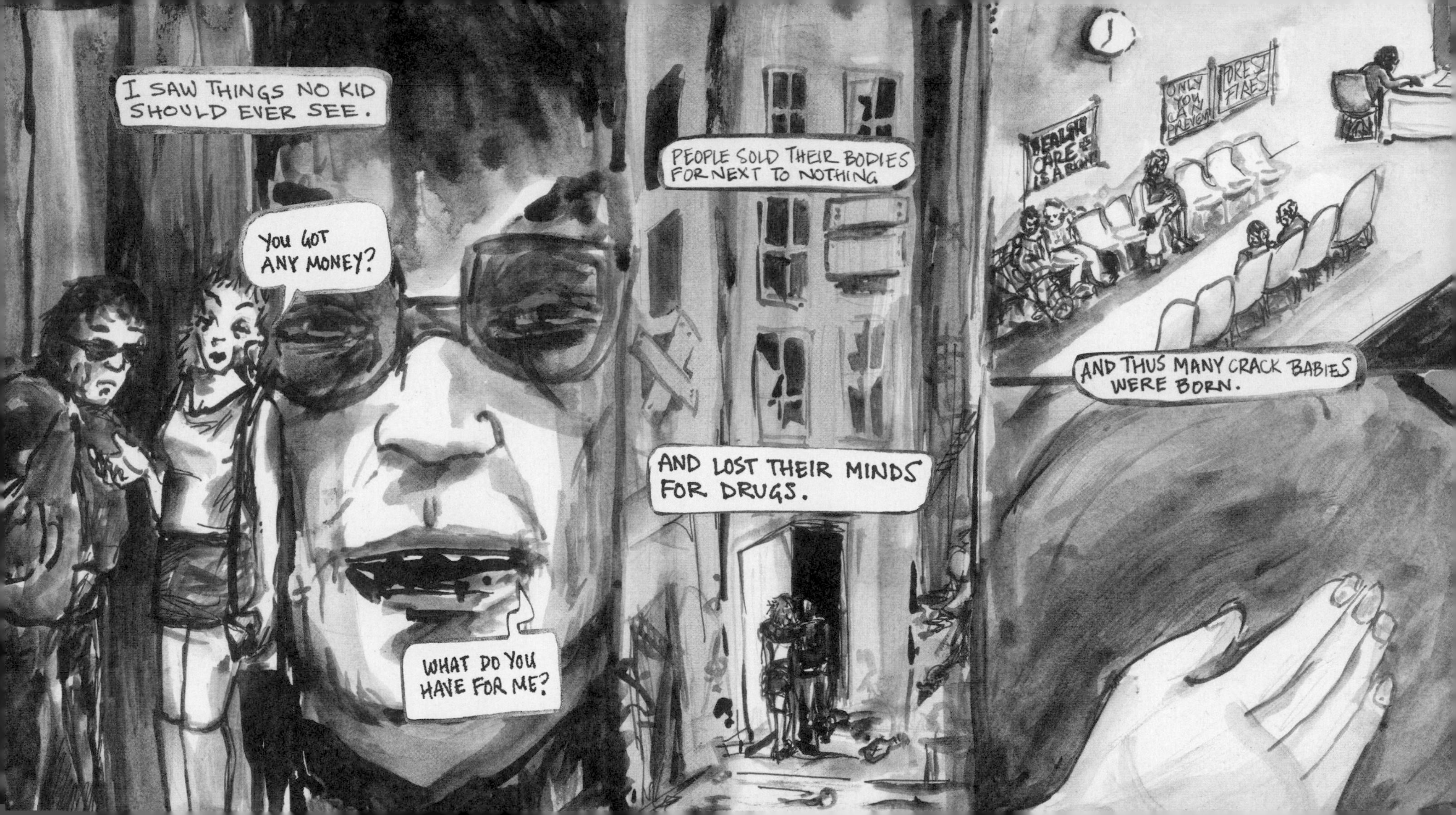
I SAW THINGS NO KID SHOULD EVER SEE.
YOU GOT ANY MONEY?
WHAT DO YOU HAVE FOR ME?
PEOPLE SOLD THEIR BODIES FOR NEXT TO NOTHING
AND LOST THEIR MINDS FOR DRUGS.
ONLY YOU CAN PREVENT
FOREST FIRES
AND THUS MANY CRACK BABIES WERE BORN.

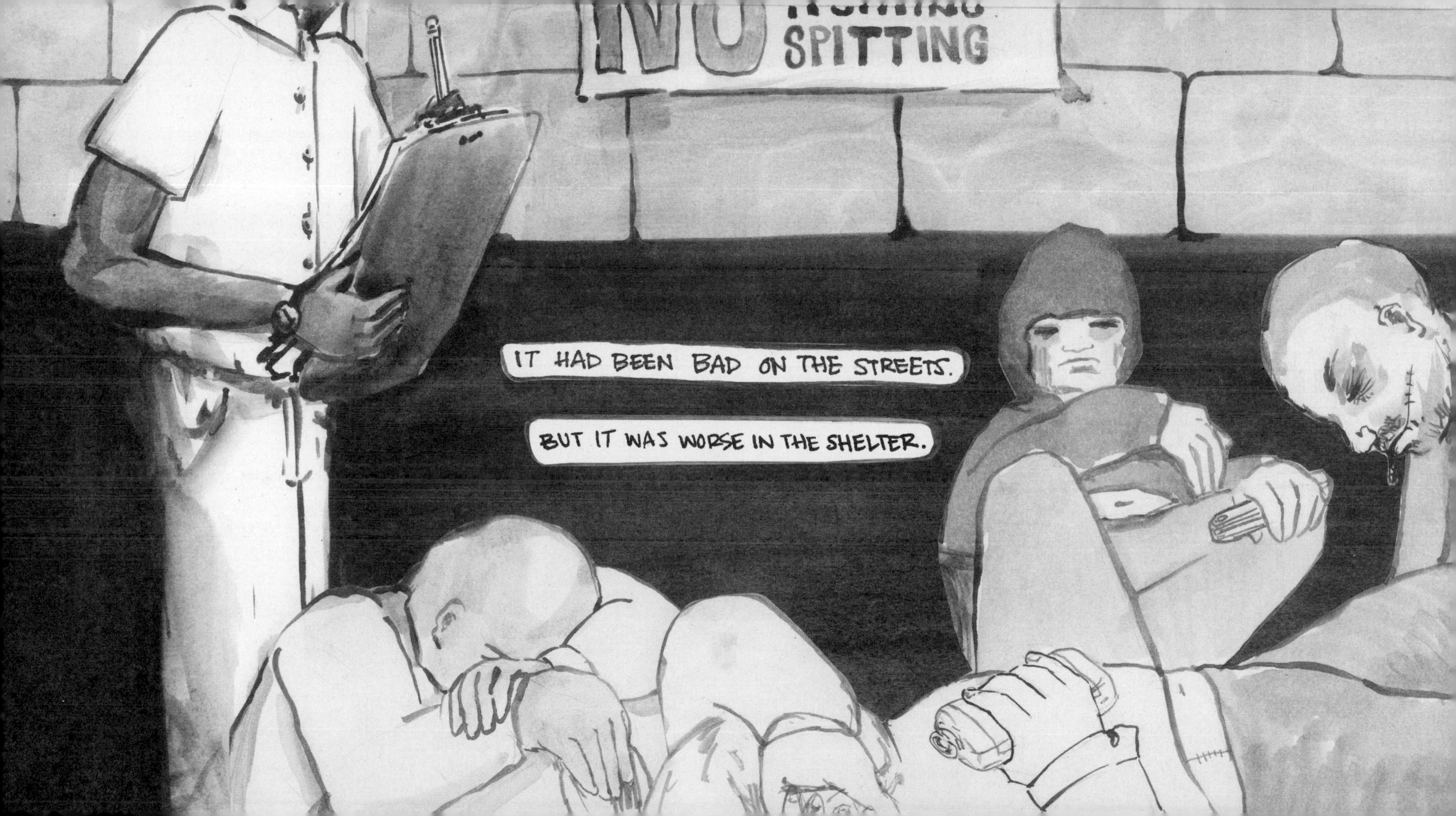
NO
SPITTING
IT HAD BEEN BAD ON THE STREETS.
BUT IT WAS WORSE IN THE SHELTER.

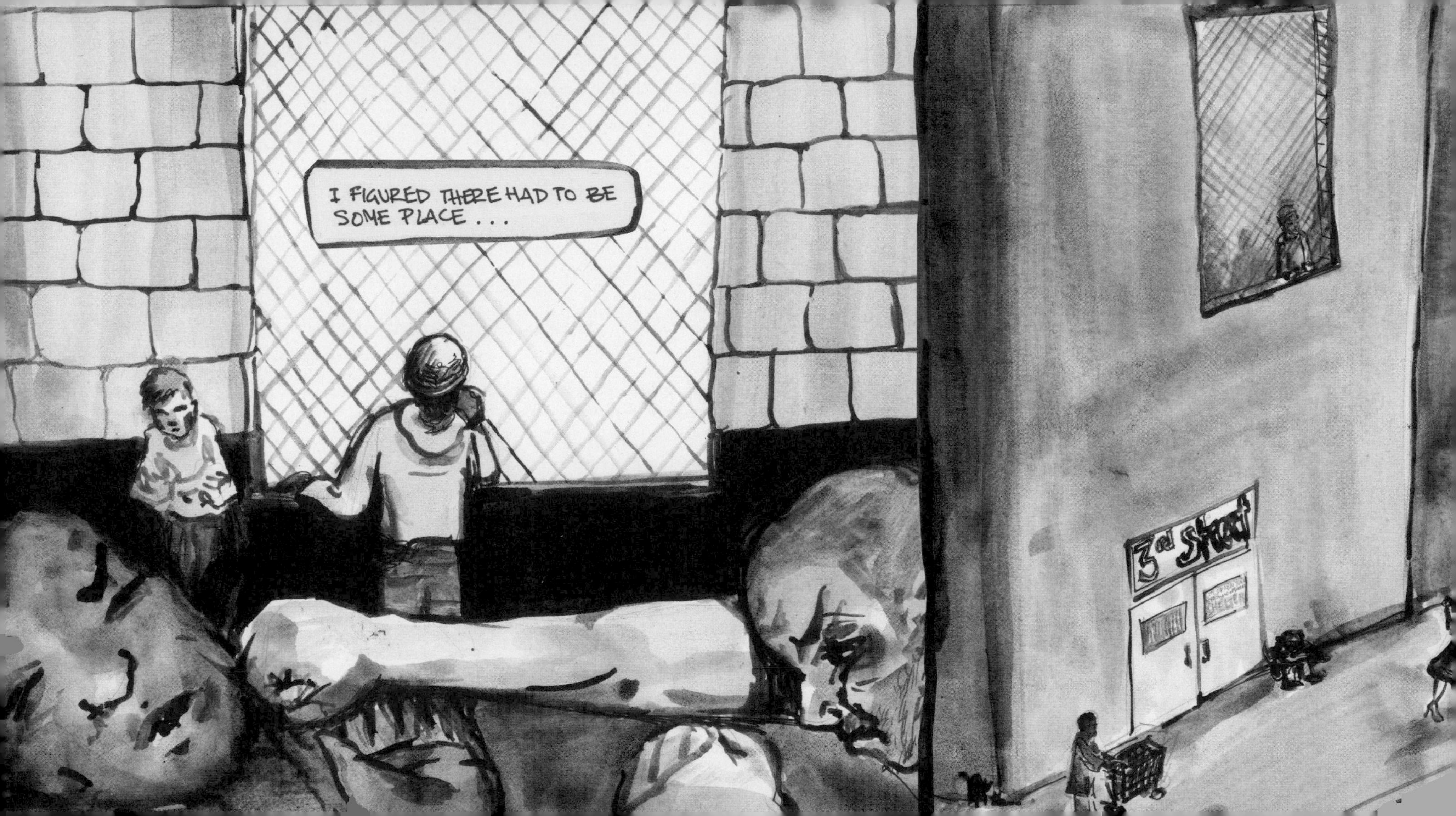
I FIGURED THERE HAD TO BE SOME PLACE . . .
3rd Street

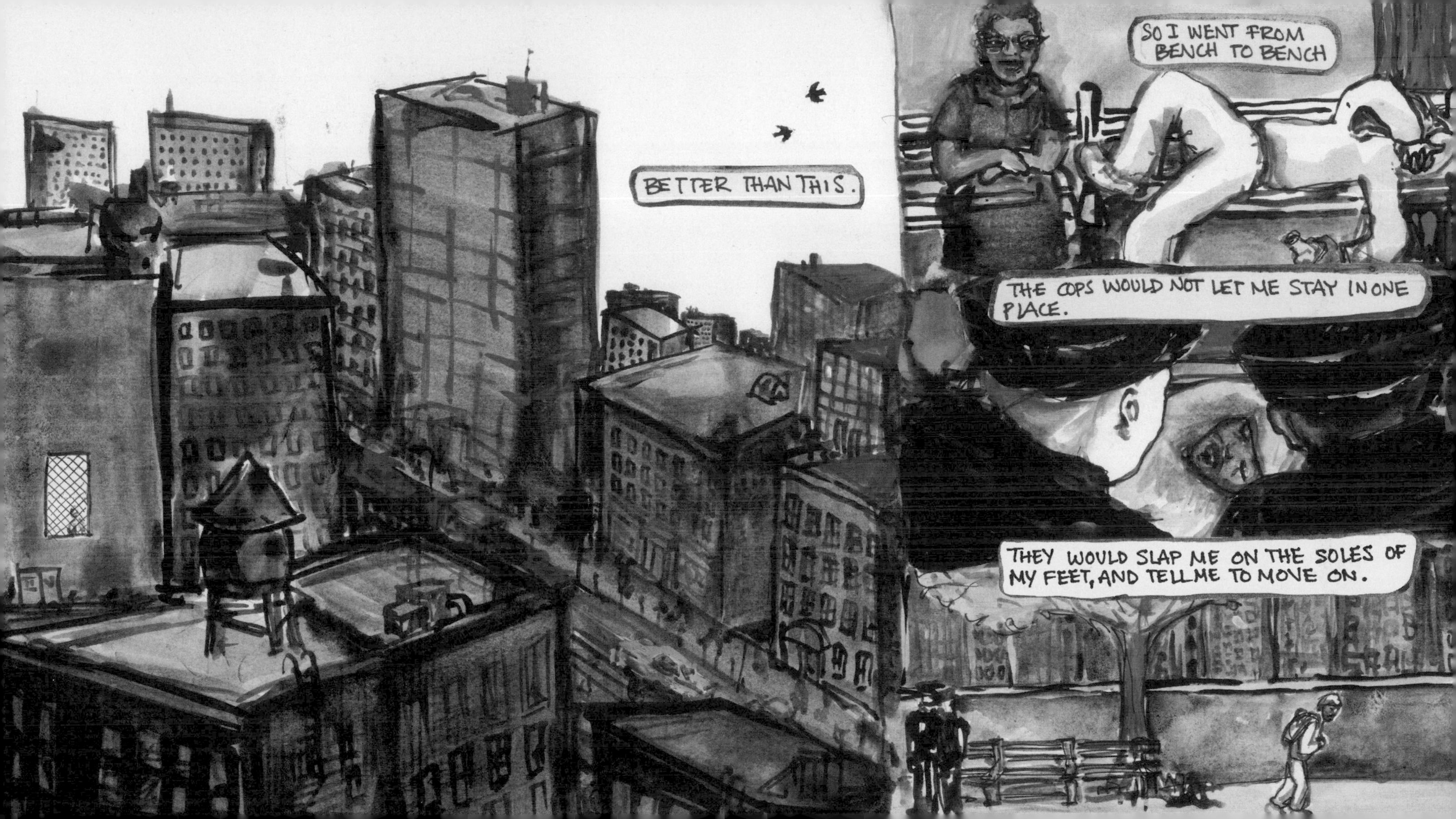
BETTER THAN THIS.
SO I WENT FROM BENCH TO BENCH
THE COPS WOULD NOT LET ME STAY IN ONE PLACE.
THEY WOULD SLAP ME ON THE SOLES OF MY FEET, AND TELL ME TO MOVE ON.

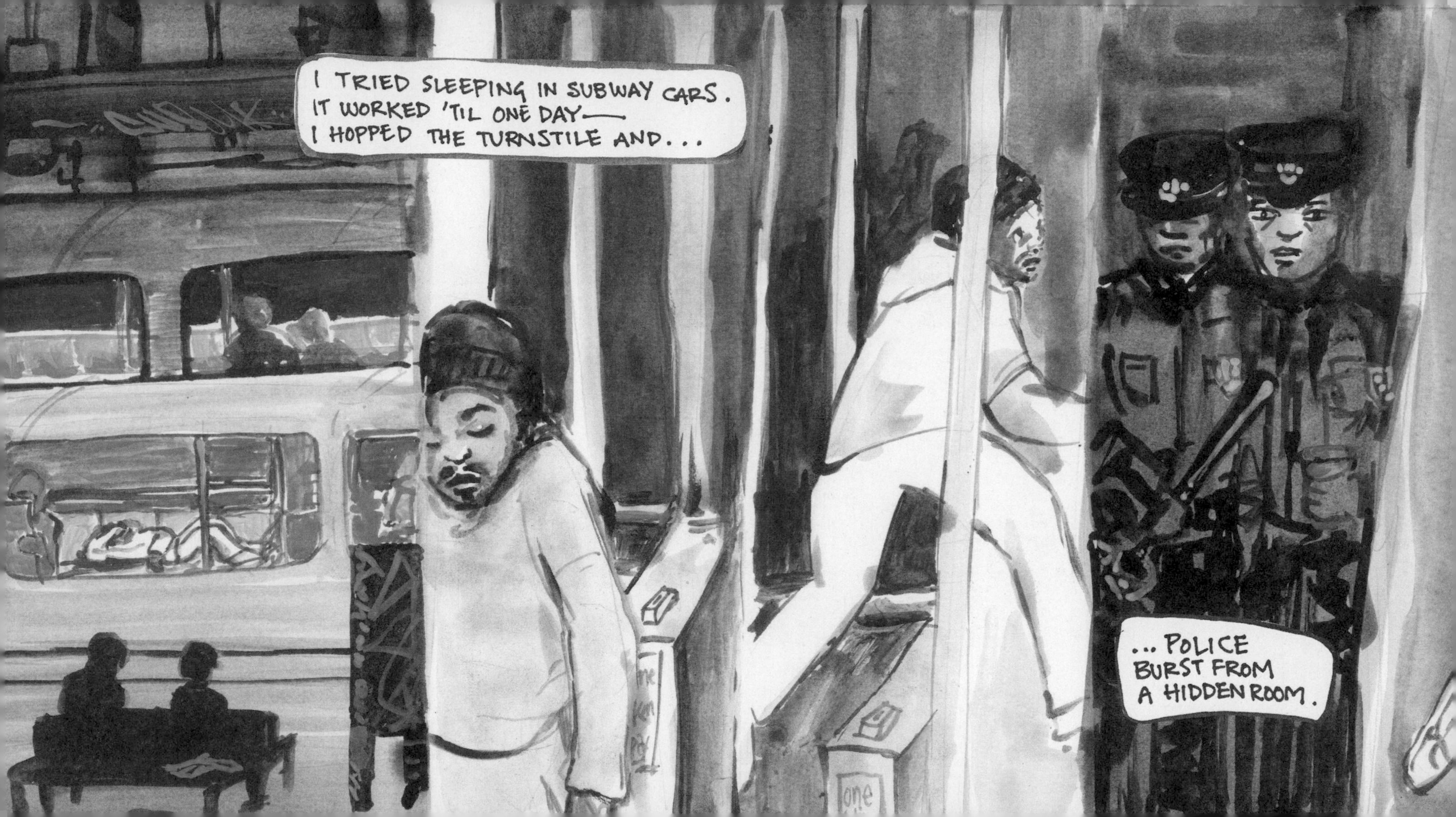
I TRIED SLEEPING IN SUBWAY CARS. IT WORKED 'TIL ONE DAY— I HOPPED THE TURNSTILE AND...
...POLICE BURST FROM A HIDDEN ROOM.

THEY CALLED ME TO COME BACK, BUT I KEPT GOING. THEY BEGAN TO CHASE ME. LET'S JUST SAY, THEY WEREN'T HAPPY. WHEN I GOT TO THE END OF THE PLATFORM THERE WAS NOWHERE TO GO BUT INTO THE TUNNEL.

Do not enter or cross tracks

Do not enter or cross tracks

Do not enter or cross tracks

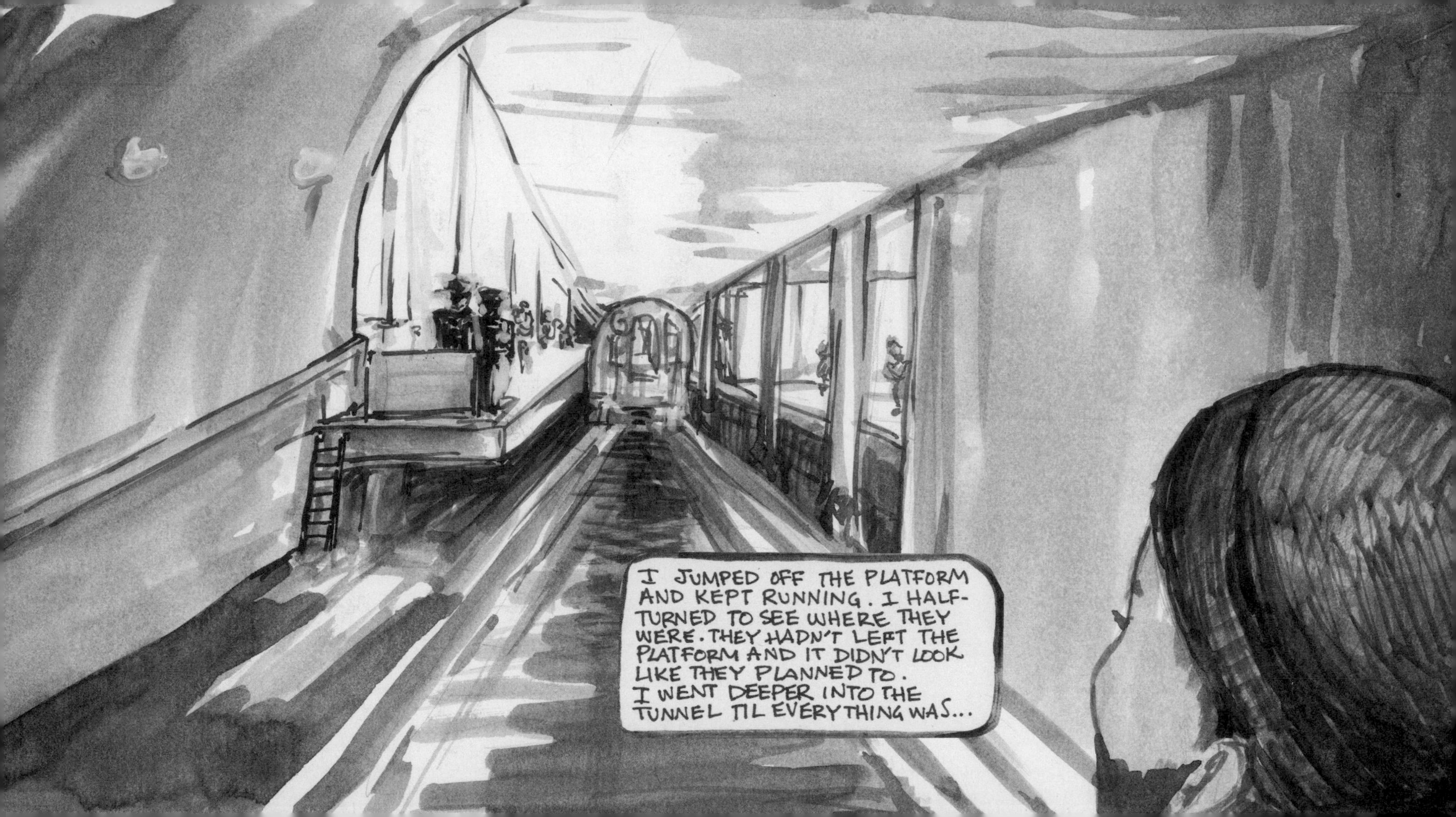
I JUMPED OFF THE PLATFORM AND KEPT RUNNING. I HALF-TURNED TO SEE WHERE THEY WERE. THEY HADN'T LEFT THE PLATFORM AND IT DIDN'T LOOK LIKE THEY PLANNED TO. I WENT DEEPER INTO THE TUNNEL TIL EVERYTHING WAS...

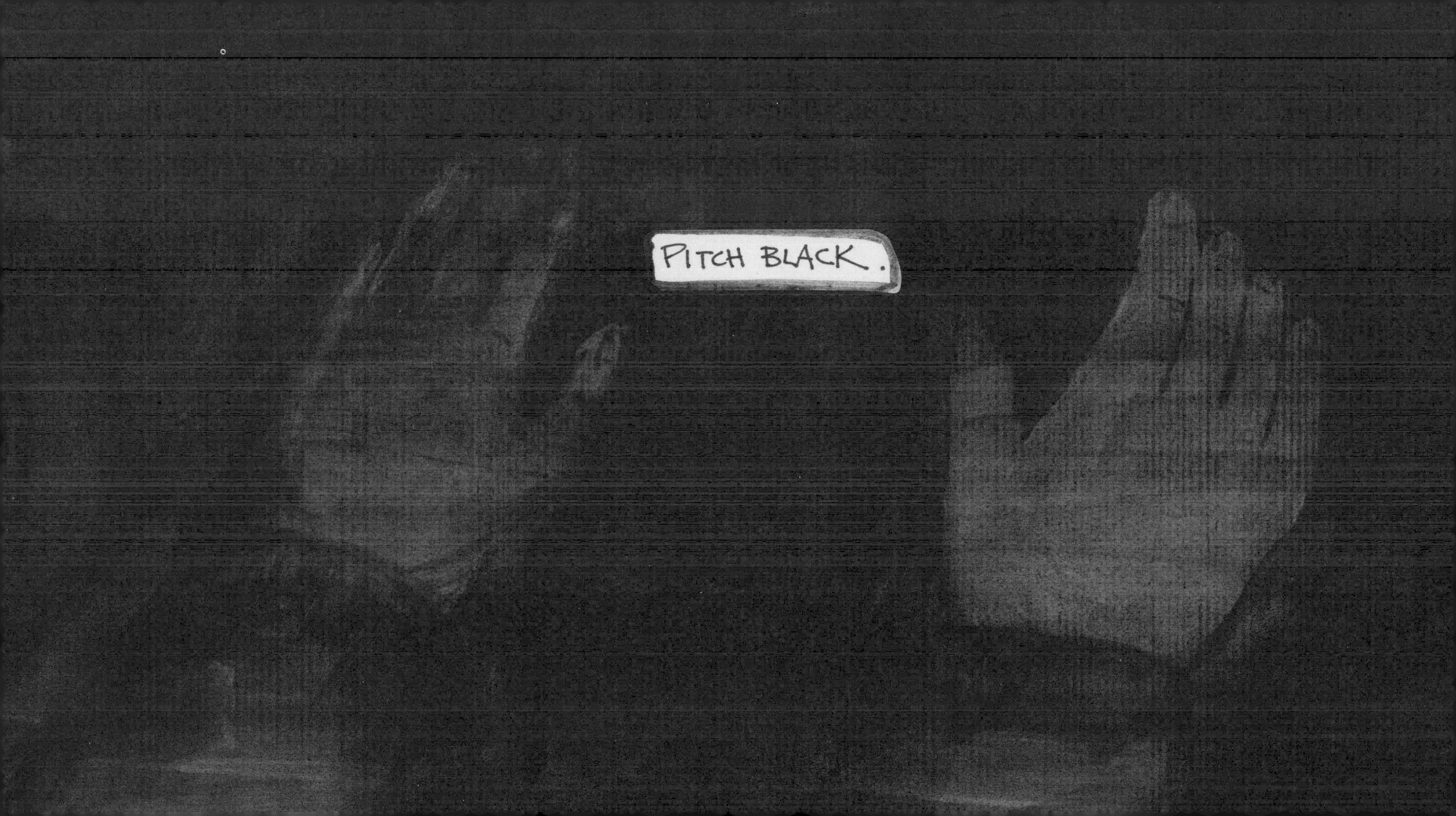
PITCH BLACK.

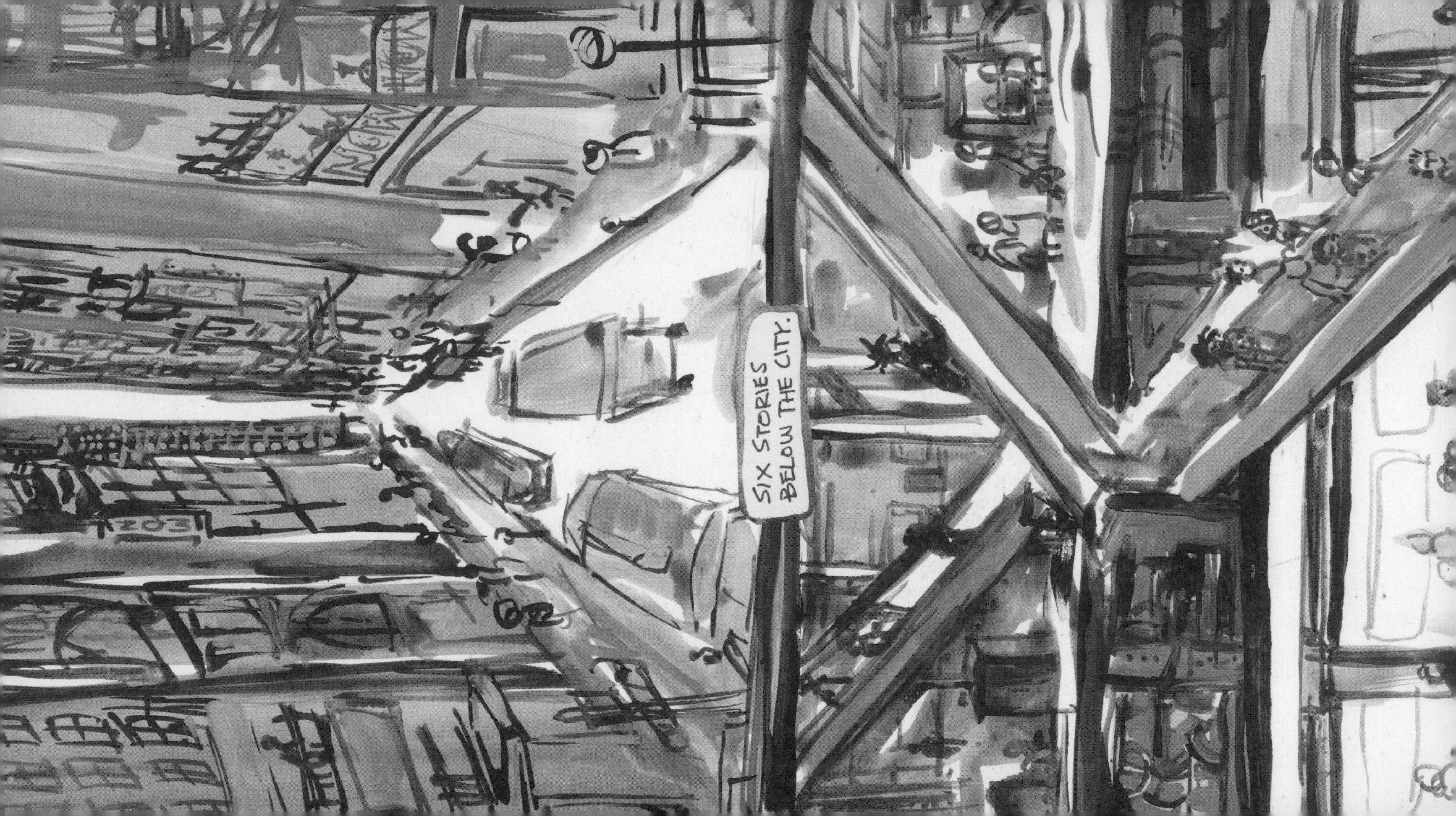
SIX STORIES
BELOW THE CITY.
203

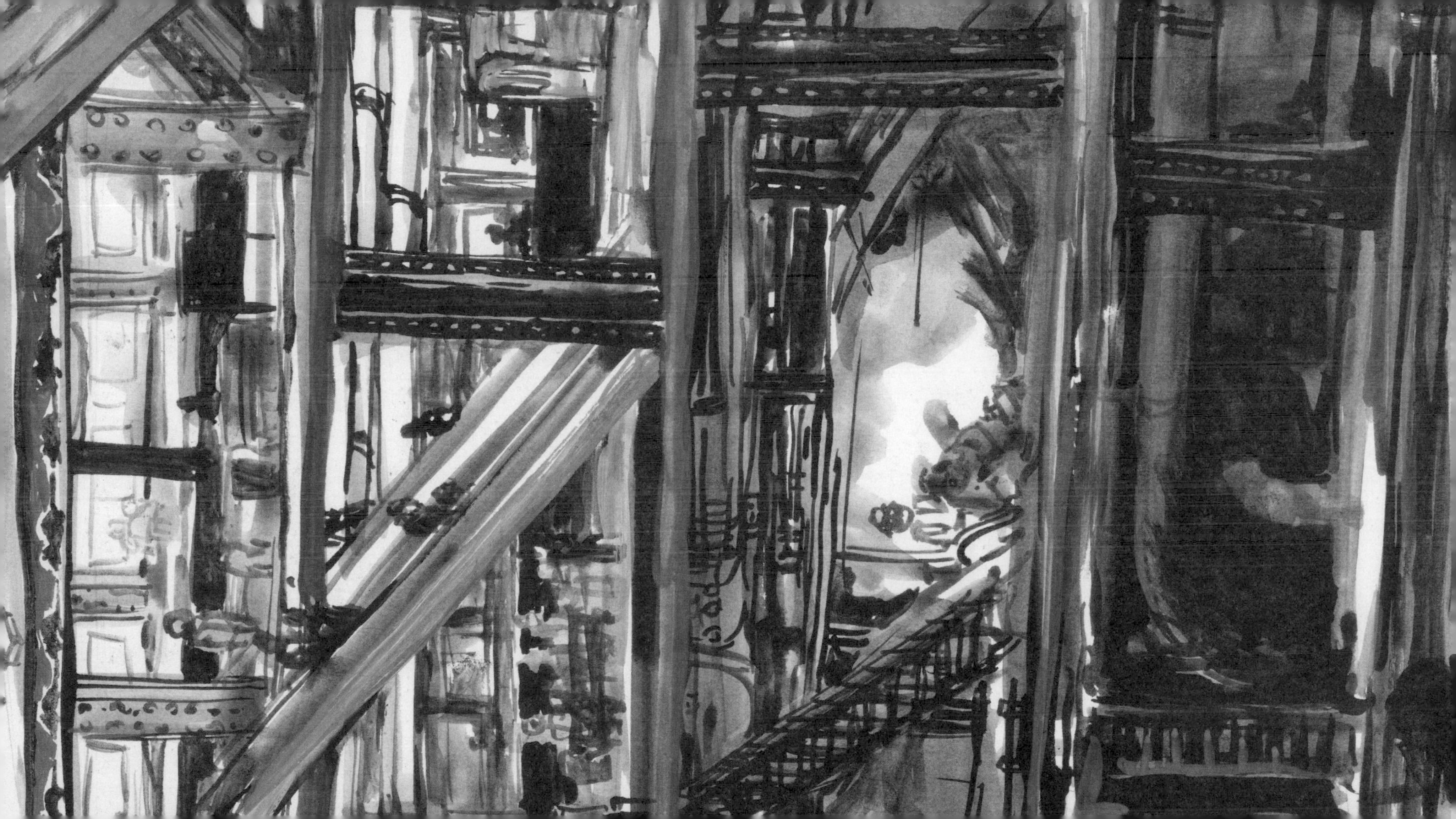

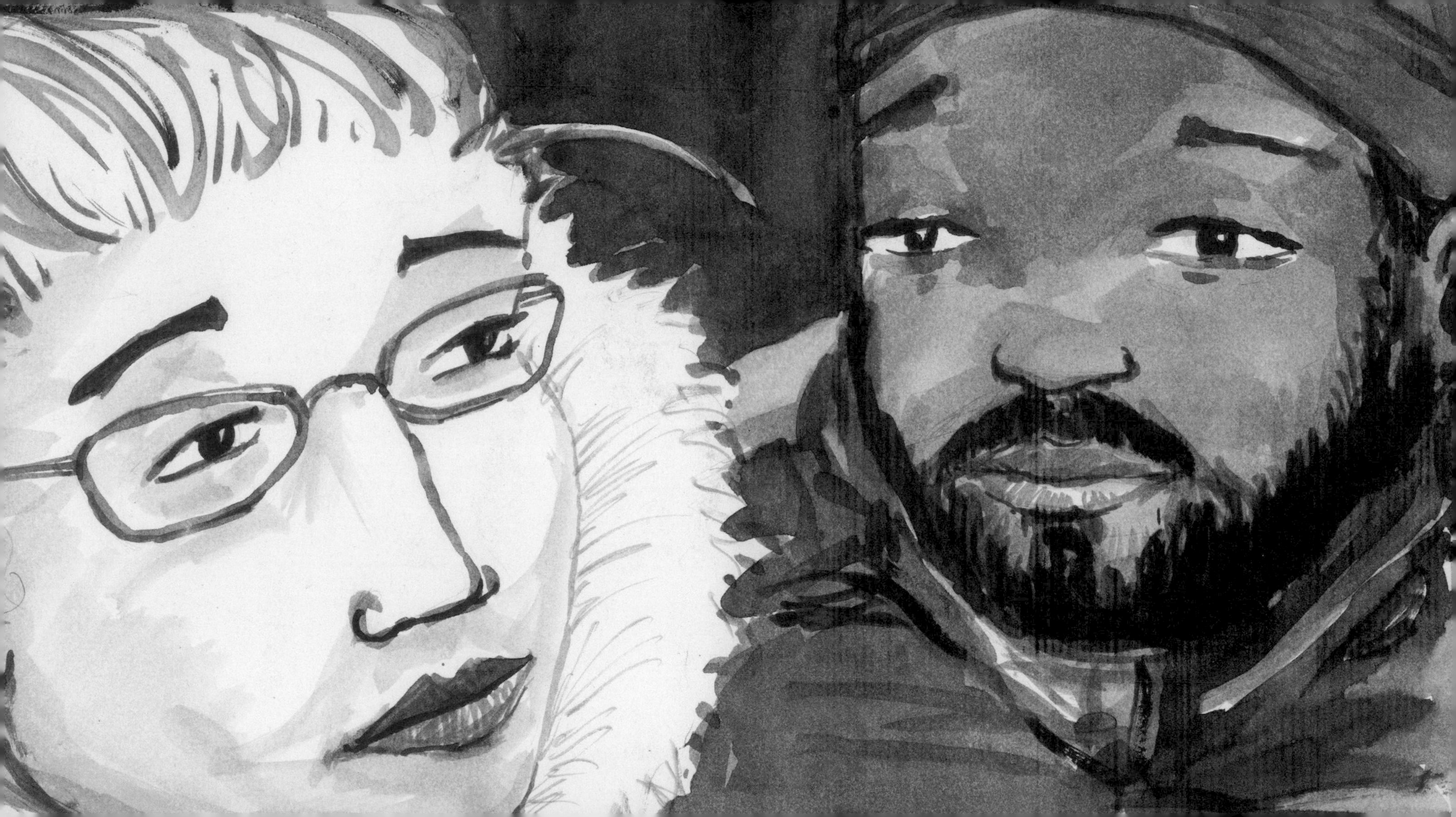

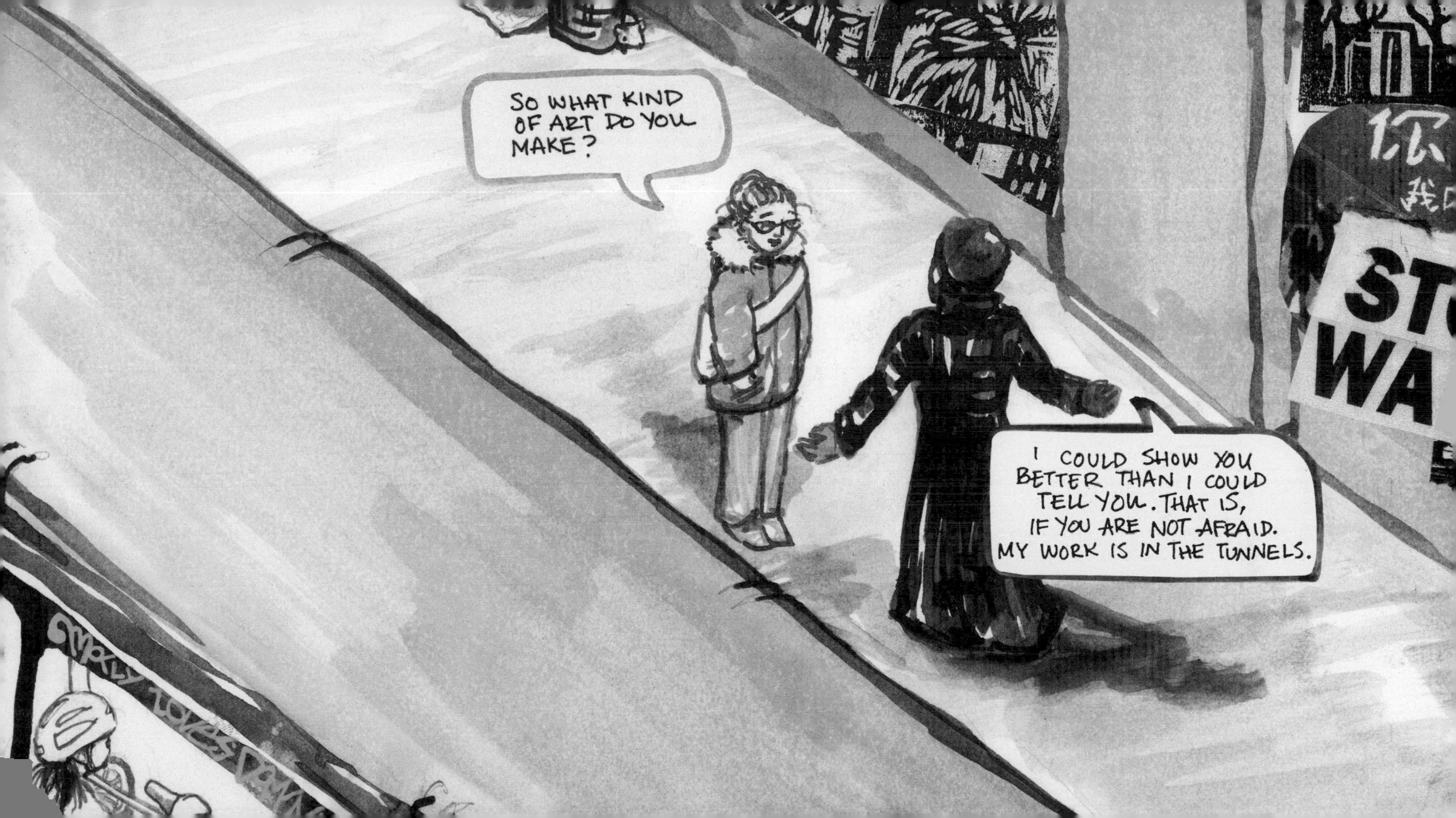
SO WHAT KIND OF ART DO YOU MAKE?
I COULD SHOW YOU BETTER THAN I COULD TELL YOU. THAT IS, IF YOU ARE NOT AFRAID. MY WORK IS IN THE TUNNELS.

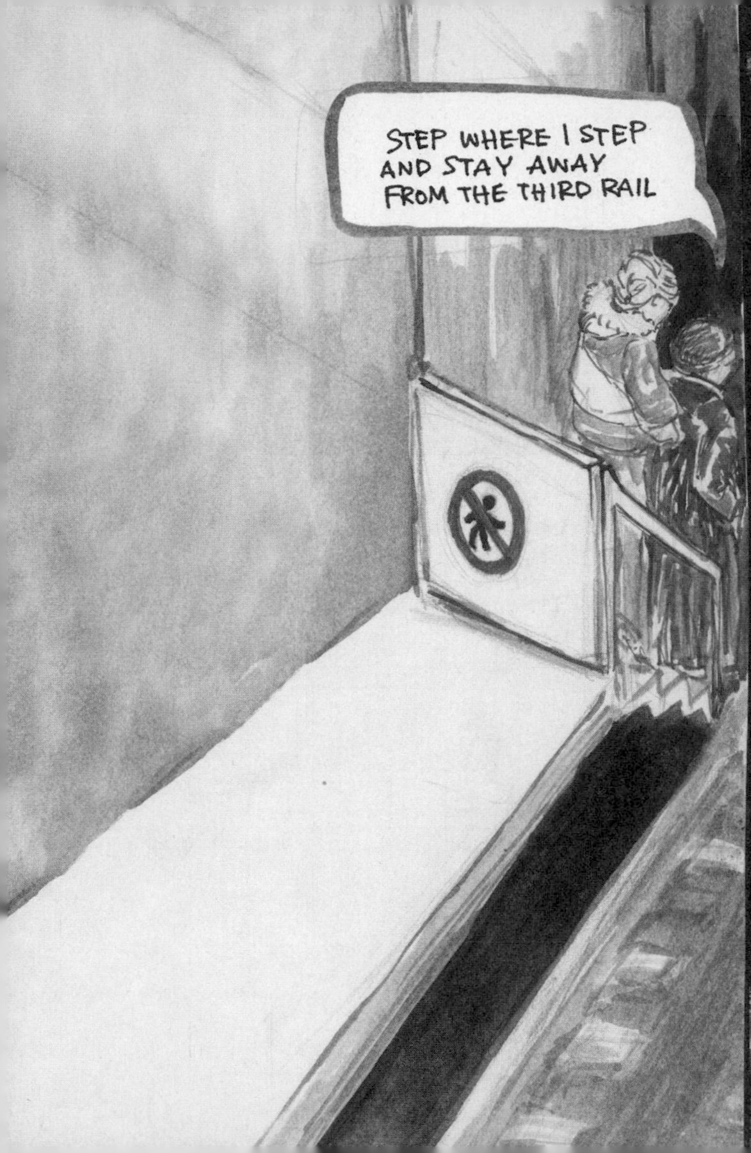
STEP WHERE I STEP AND STAY AWAY FROM THE THIRD RAIL

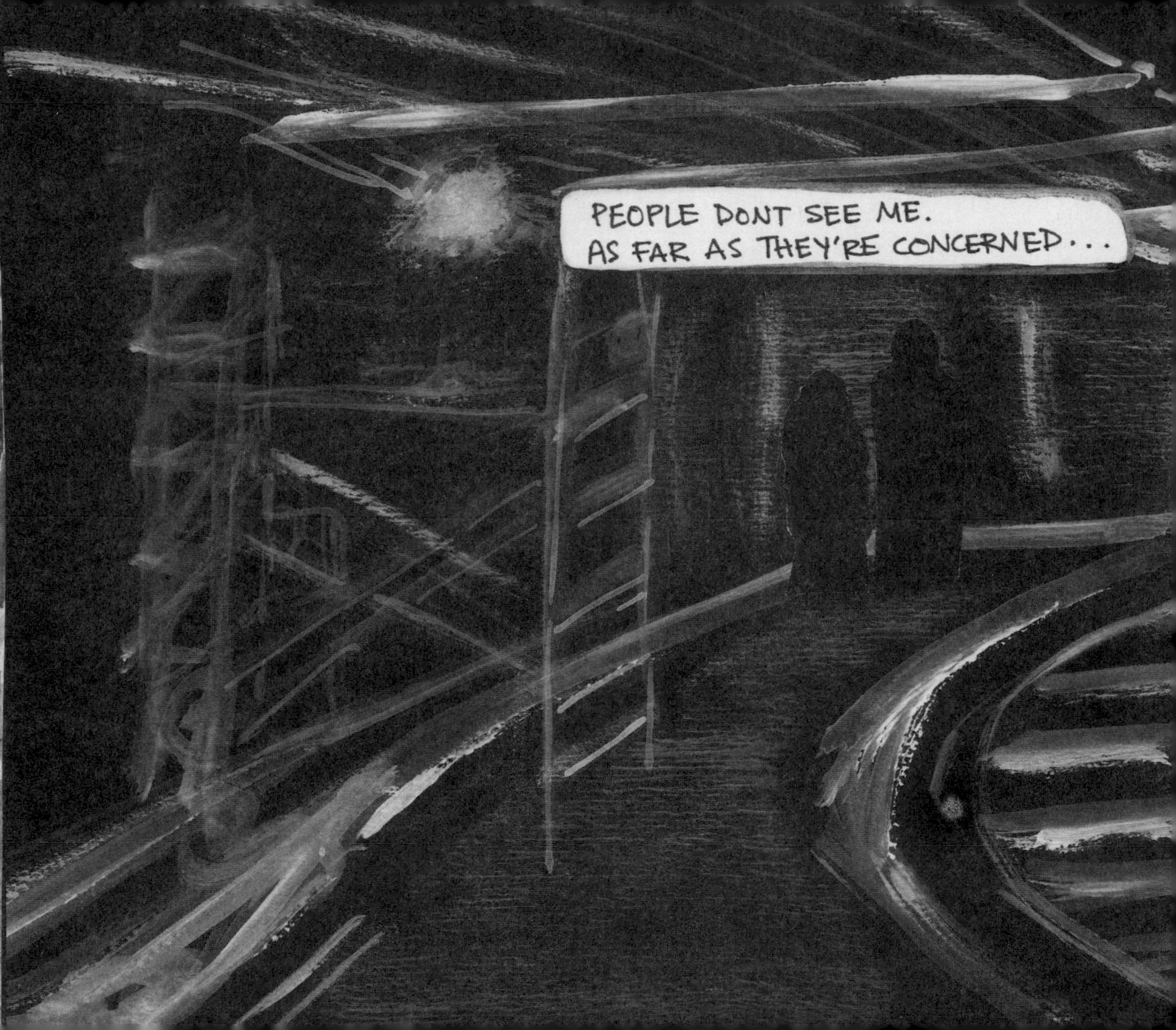
PEOPLE DONT SEE ME. AS FAR AS THEY'RE CONCERNED . . .

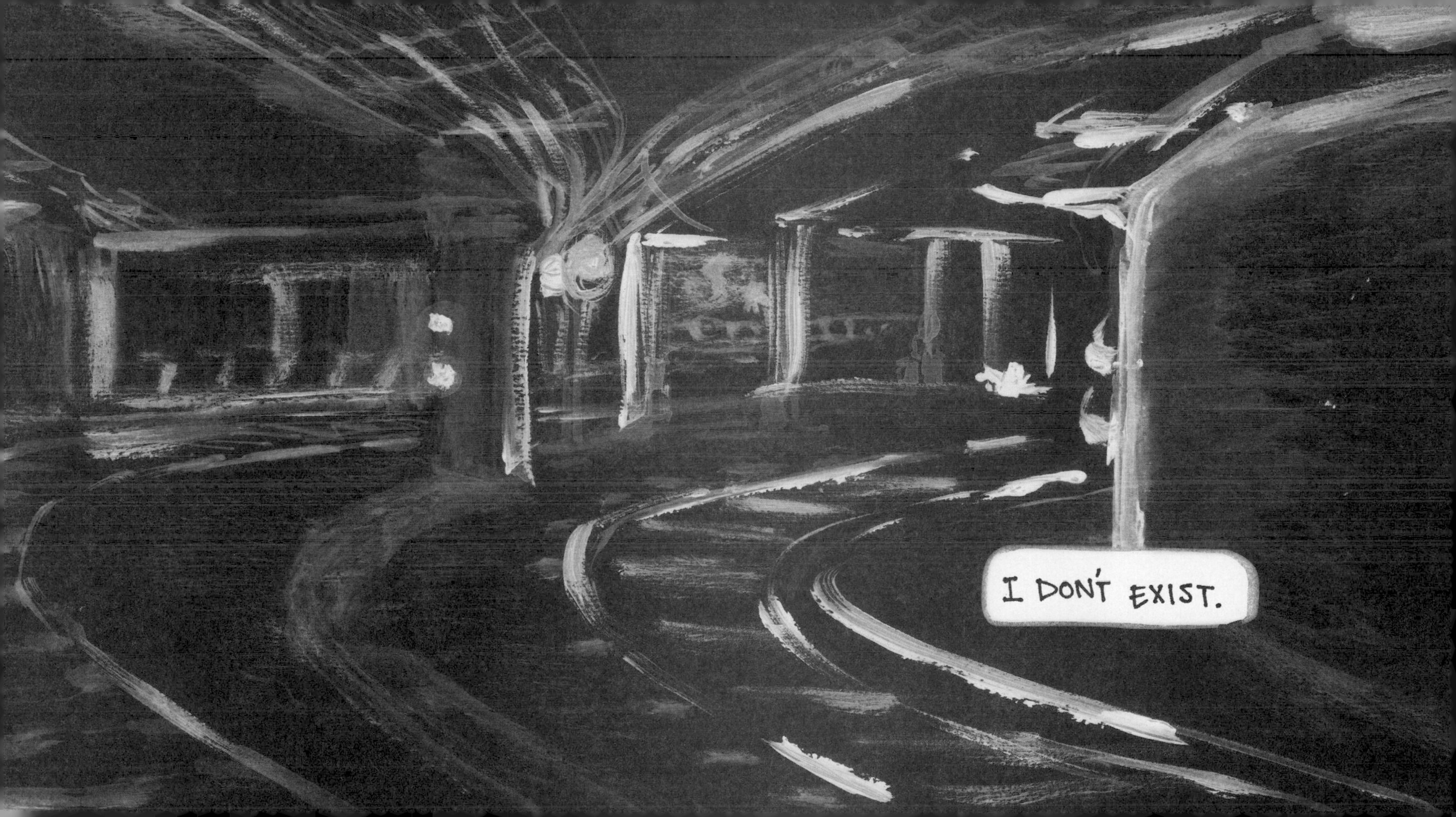
I DON'T EXIST.

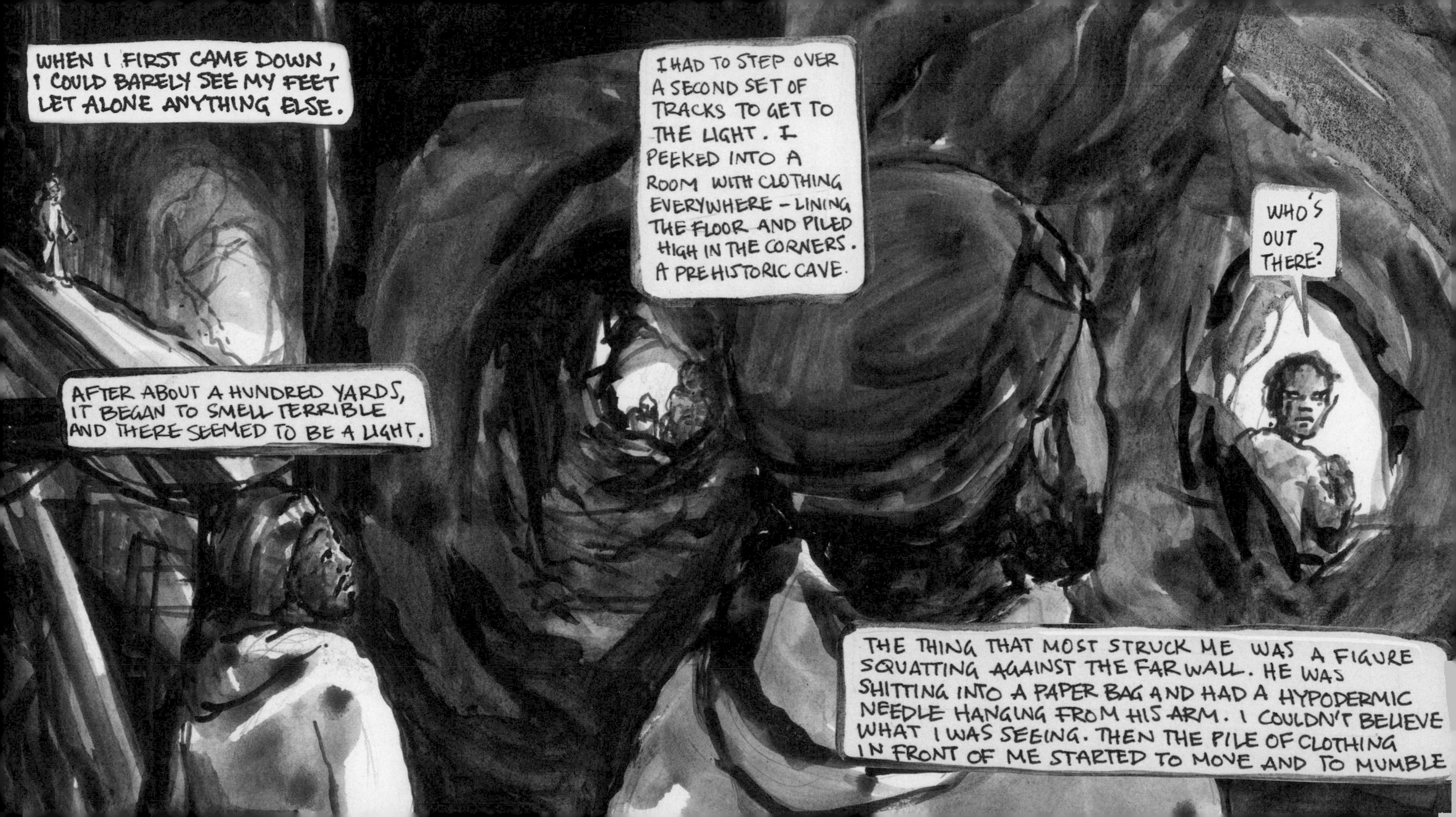
WHEN I FIRST CAME DOWN, I COULD BARELY SEE MY FEET LET ALONE ANYTHING ELSE.
AFTER ABOUT A HUNDRED YARDS, IT BEGAN TO SMELL TERRIBLE AND THERE SEEMED TO BE A LIGHT.
I HAD TO STEP OVER A SECOND SET OF TRACKS TO GET TO THE LIGHT. I PEEKED INTO A ROOM WITH CLOTHING EVERYWHERE – LINING THE FLOOR AND PILED HIGH IN THE CORNERS. A PREHISTORIC CAVE.
WHO'S OUT THERE?
THE THING THAT MOST STRUCK ME WAS A FIGURE SQUATTING AGAINST THE FAR WALL. HE WAS SHITTING INTO A PAPER BAG AND HAD A HYPODERMIC NEEDLE HANGING FROM HIS ARM. I COULDN'T BELIEVE WHAT I WAS SEEING. THEN THE PILE OF CLOTHING IN FRONT OF ME STARTED TO MOVE AND TO MUMBLE

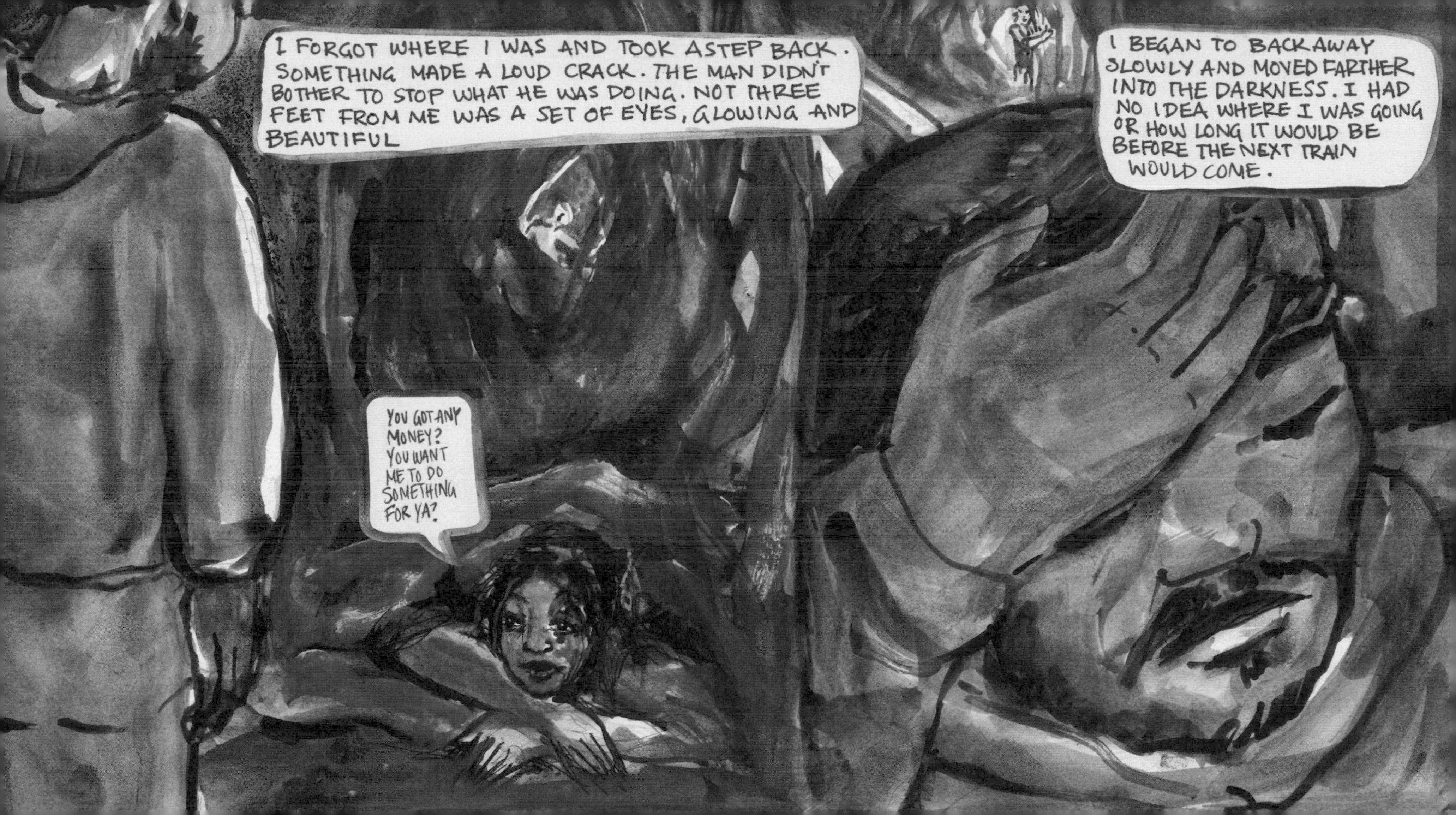
I FORGOT WHERE I WAS AND TOOK A STEP BACK. SOMETHING MADE A LOUD CRACK. THE MAN DIDN'T BOTHER TO STOP WHAT HE WAS DOING. NOT THREE FEET FROM ME WAS A SET OF EYES, GLOWING AND BEAUTIFUL
YOU GOT ANY MONEY? YOU WANT ME TO DO SOMETHING FOR YA?
I BEGAN TO BACK AWAY SLOWLY AND MOVED FARTHER INTO THE DARKNESS. I HAD NO IDEA WHERE I WAS GOING OR HOW LONG IT WOULD BE BEFORE THE NEXT TRAIN WOULD COME.

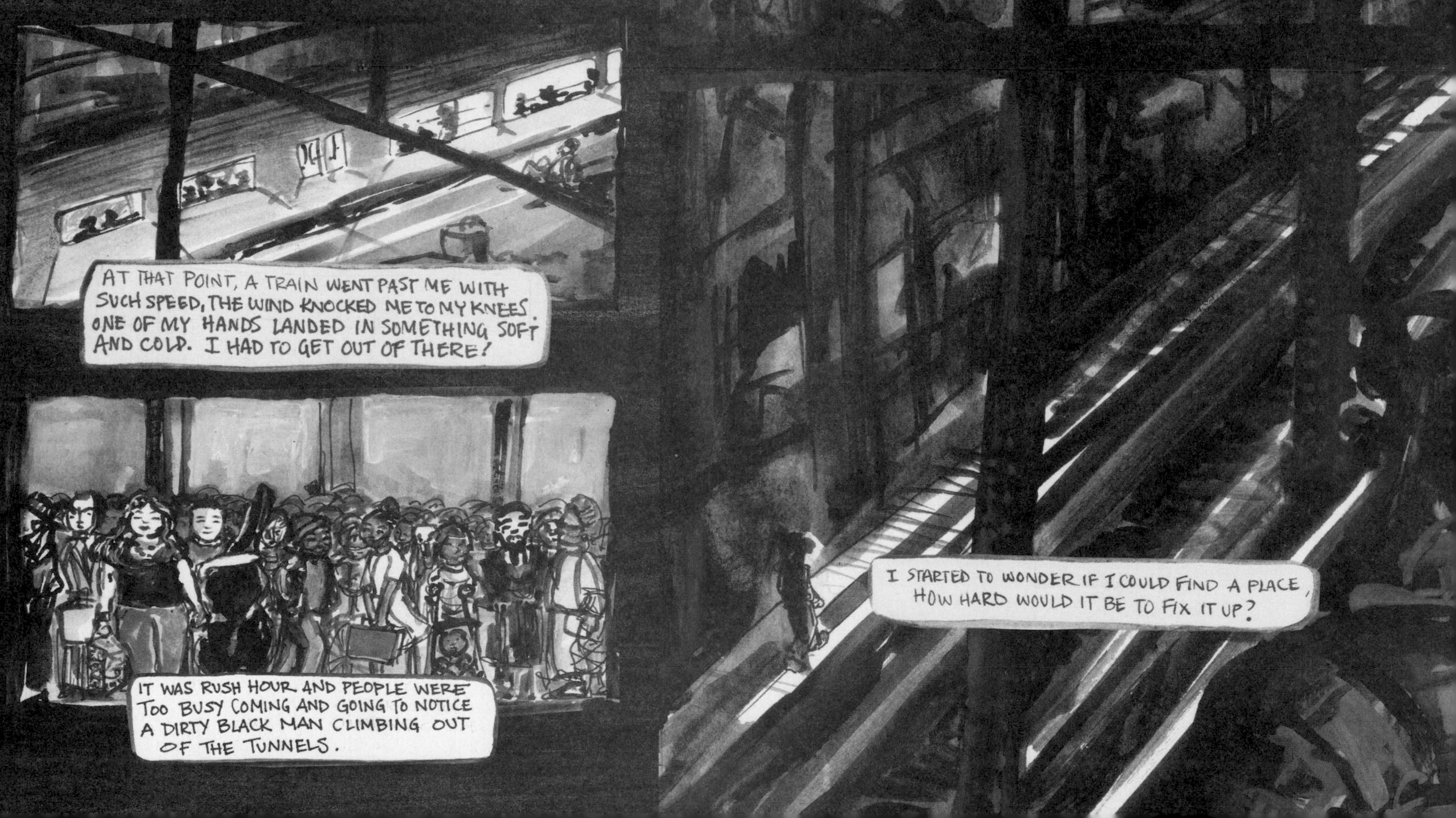
AT THAT POINT, A TRAIN WENT PAST ME WITH SUCH SPEED, THE WIND KNOCKED ME TO MY KNEES. ONE OF MY HANDS LANDED IN SOMETHING SOFT AND COLD. I HAD TO GET OUT OF THERE!
IT WAS RUSH HOUR AND PEOPLE WERE TOO BUSY COMING AND GOING TO NOTICE A DIRTY BLACK MAN CLIMBING OUT OF THE TUNNELS.
I STARTED TO WONDER IF I COULD FIND A PLACE, HOW HARD WOULD IT BE TO FIX IT UP?

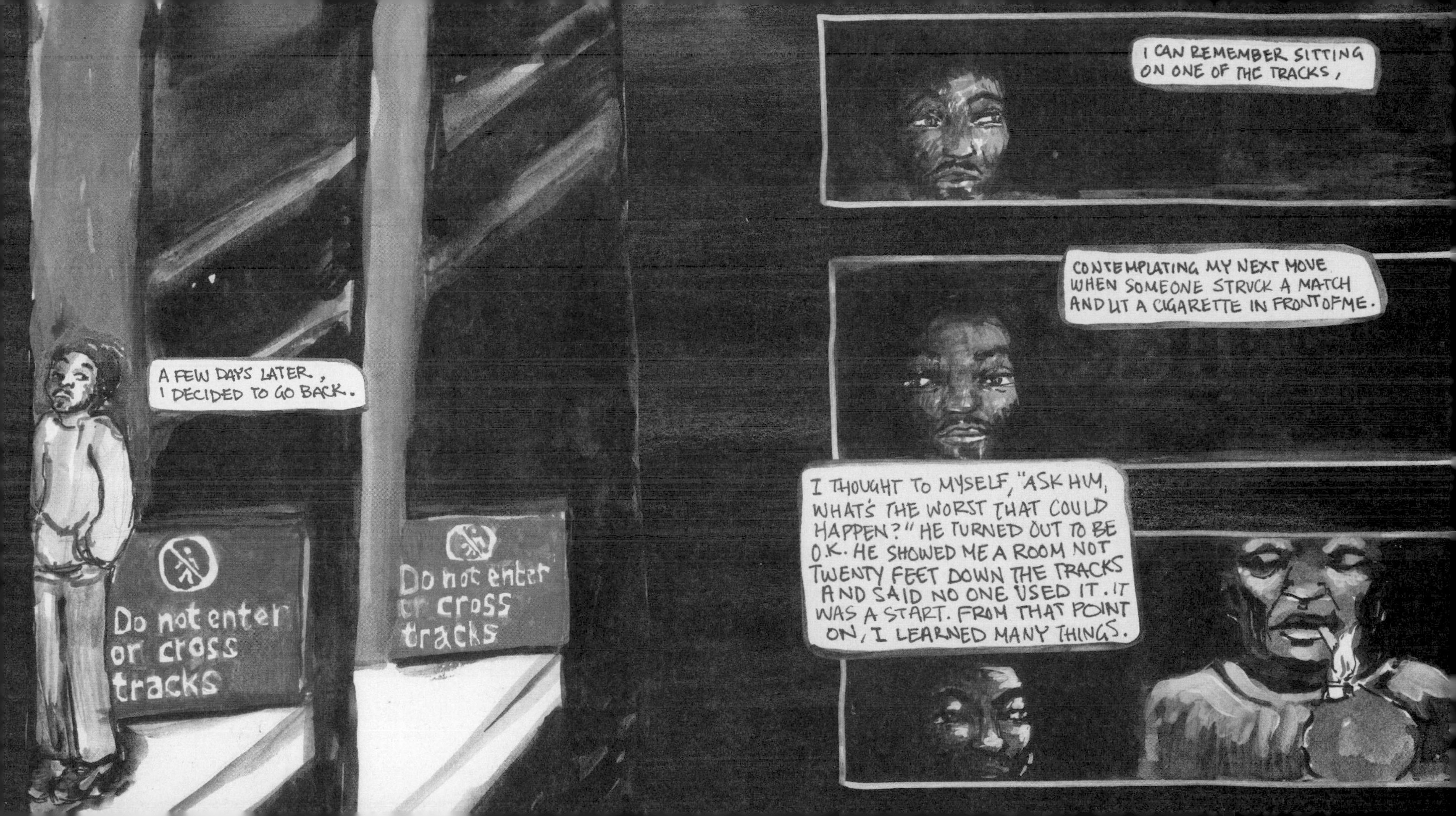
A FEW DAYS LATER, I DECIDED TO GO BACK.
Do not enter or cross tracks
Do not enter or cross tracks
I CAN REMEMBER SITTING ON ONE OF THE TRACKS,
CONTEMPLATING MY NEXT MOVE WHEN SOMEONE STRUCK A MATCH AND LIT A CIGARETTE IN FRONT OF ME.
I THOUGHT TO MYSELF, "ASK HIM, WHAT'S THE WORST THAT COULD HAPPEN?" HE TURNED OUT TO BE O.K. HE SHOWED ME A ROOM NOT TWENTY FEET DOWN THE TRACKS AND SAID NO ONE USED IT. IT WAS A START. FROM THAT POINT ON, I LEARNED MANY THINGS.

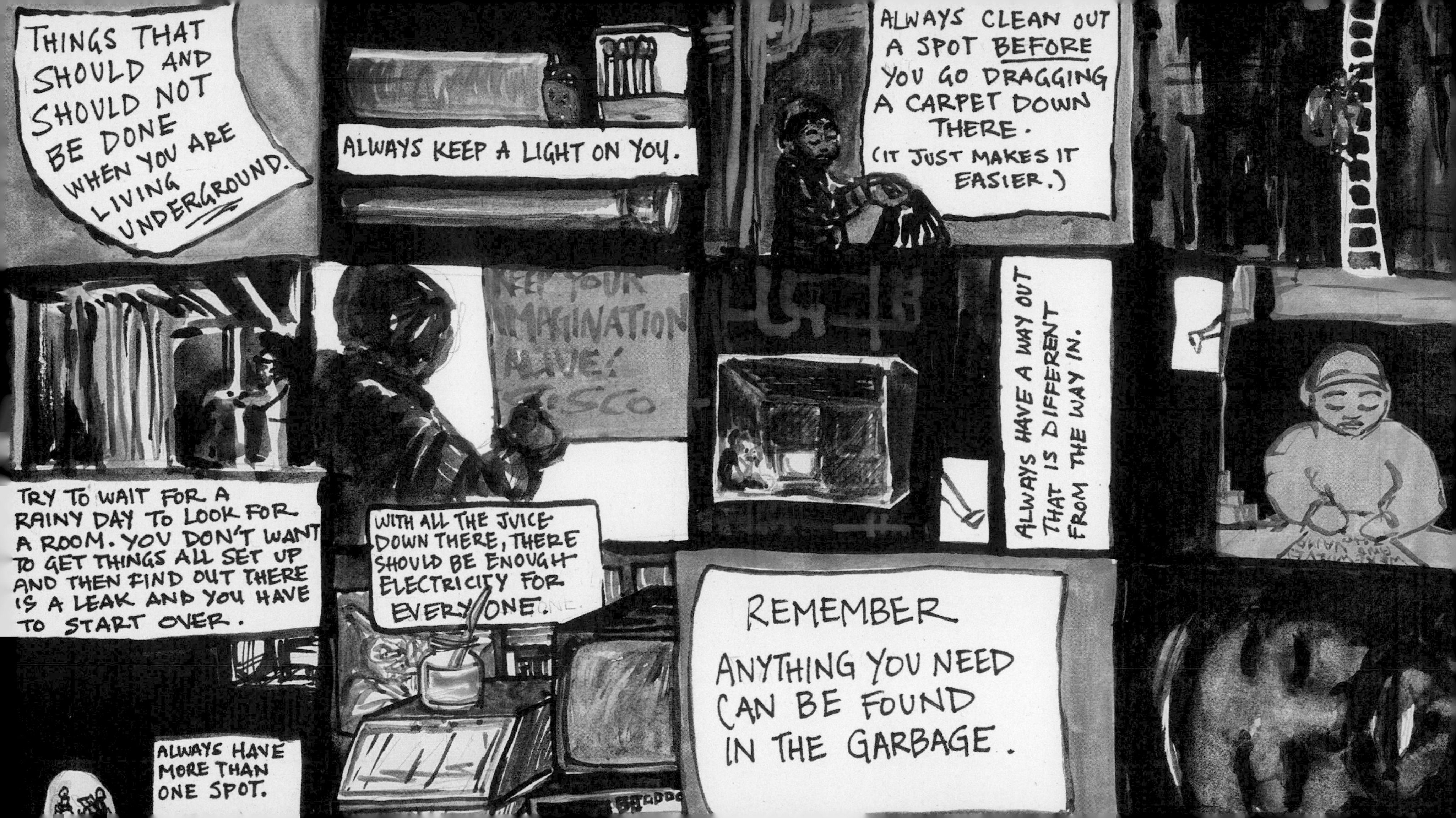
THINGS THAT SHOULD AND SHOULD NOT BE DONE WHEN YOU ARE LIVING UNDERGROUND.
ALWAYS KEEP A LIGHT ON YOU.
ALWAYS CLEAN OUT A SPOT BEFORE YOU GO DRAGGING A CARPET DOWN THERE. (IT JUST MAKES IT EASIER.)
TRY TO WAIT FOR A RAINY DAY TO LOOK FOR A ROOM. YOU DON'T WANT TO GET THINGS ALL SET UP AND THEN FIND OUT THERE IS A LEAK AND YOU HAVE TO START OVER.
IMAGINATION ALIVE!
WITH ALL THE JUICE DOWN THERE, THERE SHOULD BE ENOUGH ELECTRICITY FOR EVERYONE.
ALWAYS HAVE A WAY OUT THAT IS DIFFERENT FROM THE WAY IN.
REMEMBER
ANYTHING YOU NEED CAN BE FOUND IN THE GARBAGE.
ALWAYS HAVE MORE THAN ONE SPOT.

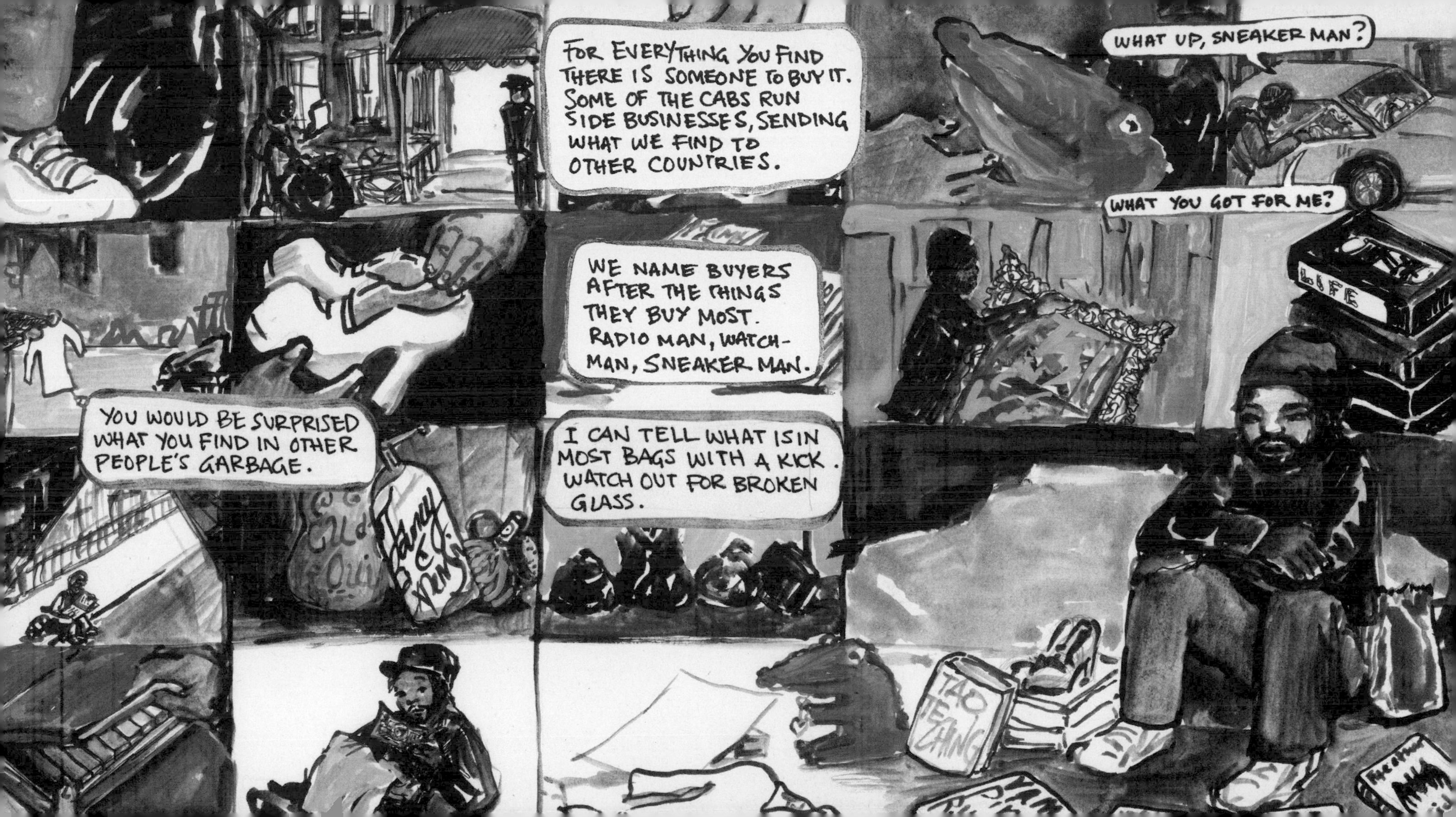

FOR EVERYTHING YOU FIND THERE IS SOMEONE TO BUY IT. SOME OF THE CABS RUN SIDE BUSINESSES, SENDING WHAT WE FIND TO OTHER COUNTRIES.
YOU WOULD BE SURPRISED WHAT YOU FIND IN OTHER PEOPLE'S GARBAGE.
WE NAME BUYERS AFTER THE THINGS THEY BUY MOST. RADIO MAN, WATCH-MAN, SNEAKER MAN.
I CAN TELL WHAT IS IN MOST BAGS WITH A KICK. WATCH OUT FOR BROKEN GLASS.
WHAT UP, SNEAKER MAN?
WHAT YOU GOT FOR ME?
LIFE
TAO TE CHING

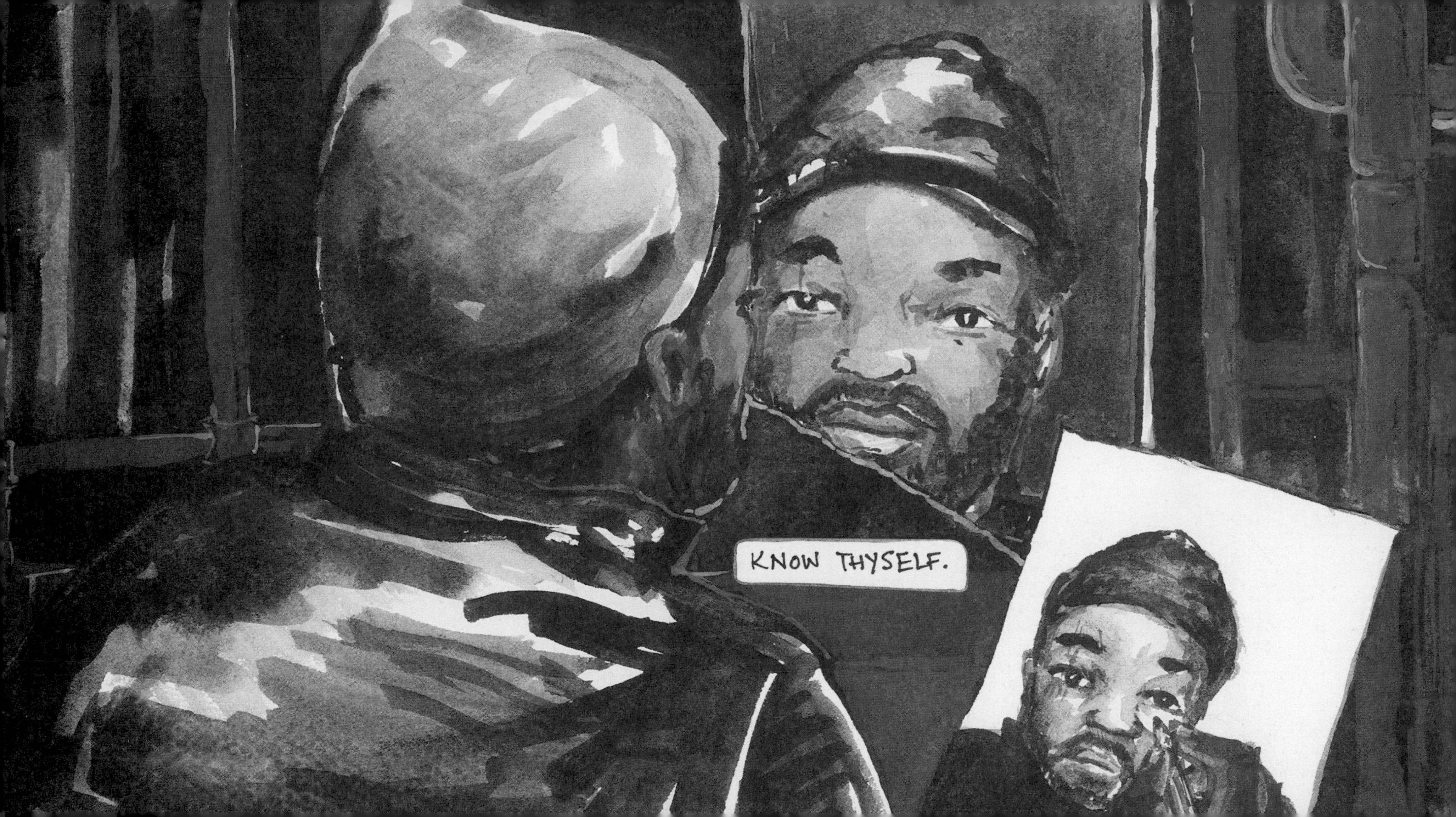
KNOW THYSELF.

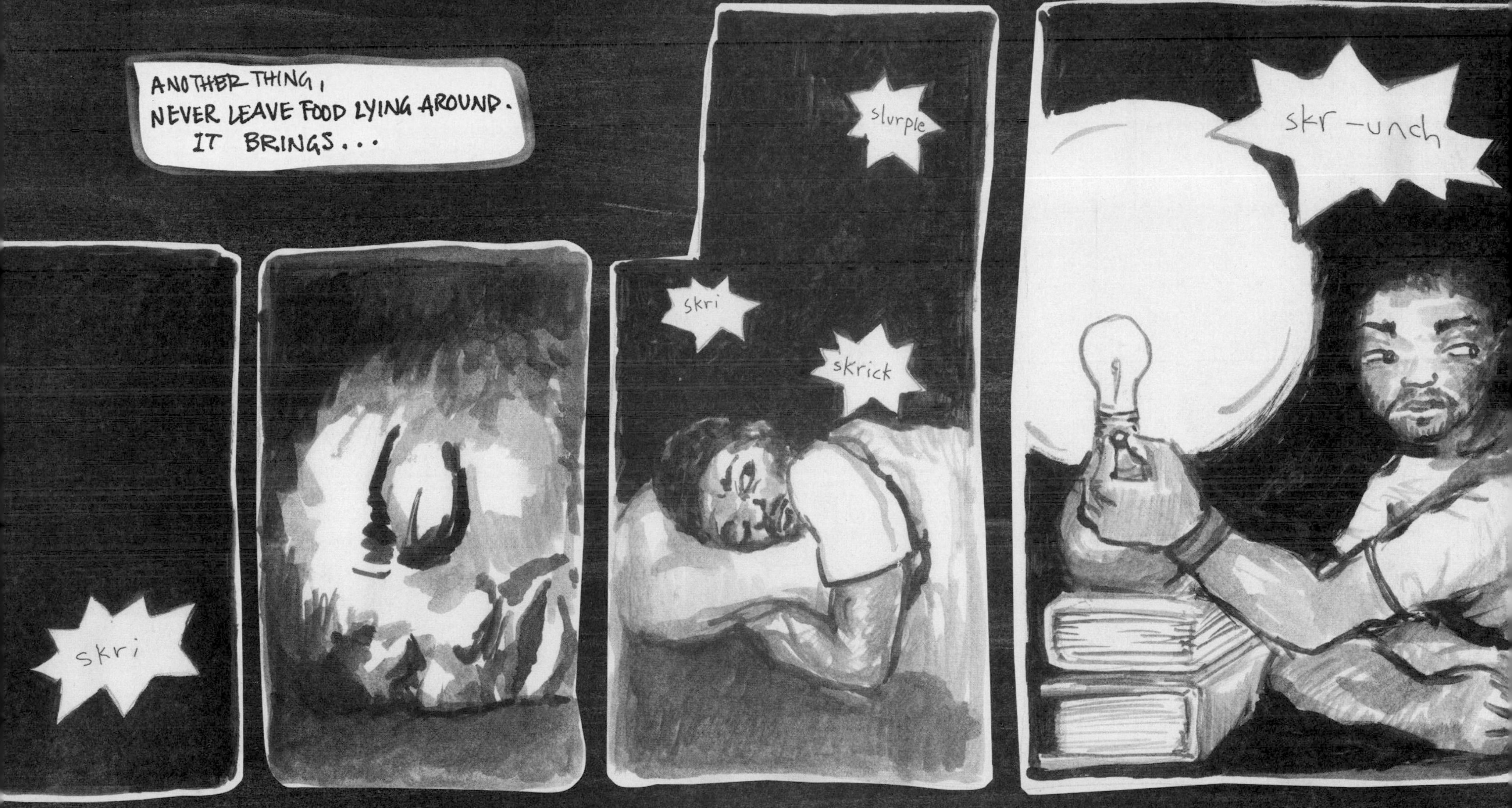
ANOTHER THING,
NEVER LEAVE FOOD LYING AROUND.
IT BRINGS . . .
skri
skri
skrick
slurple
skr-unch

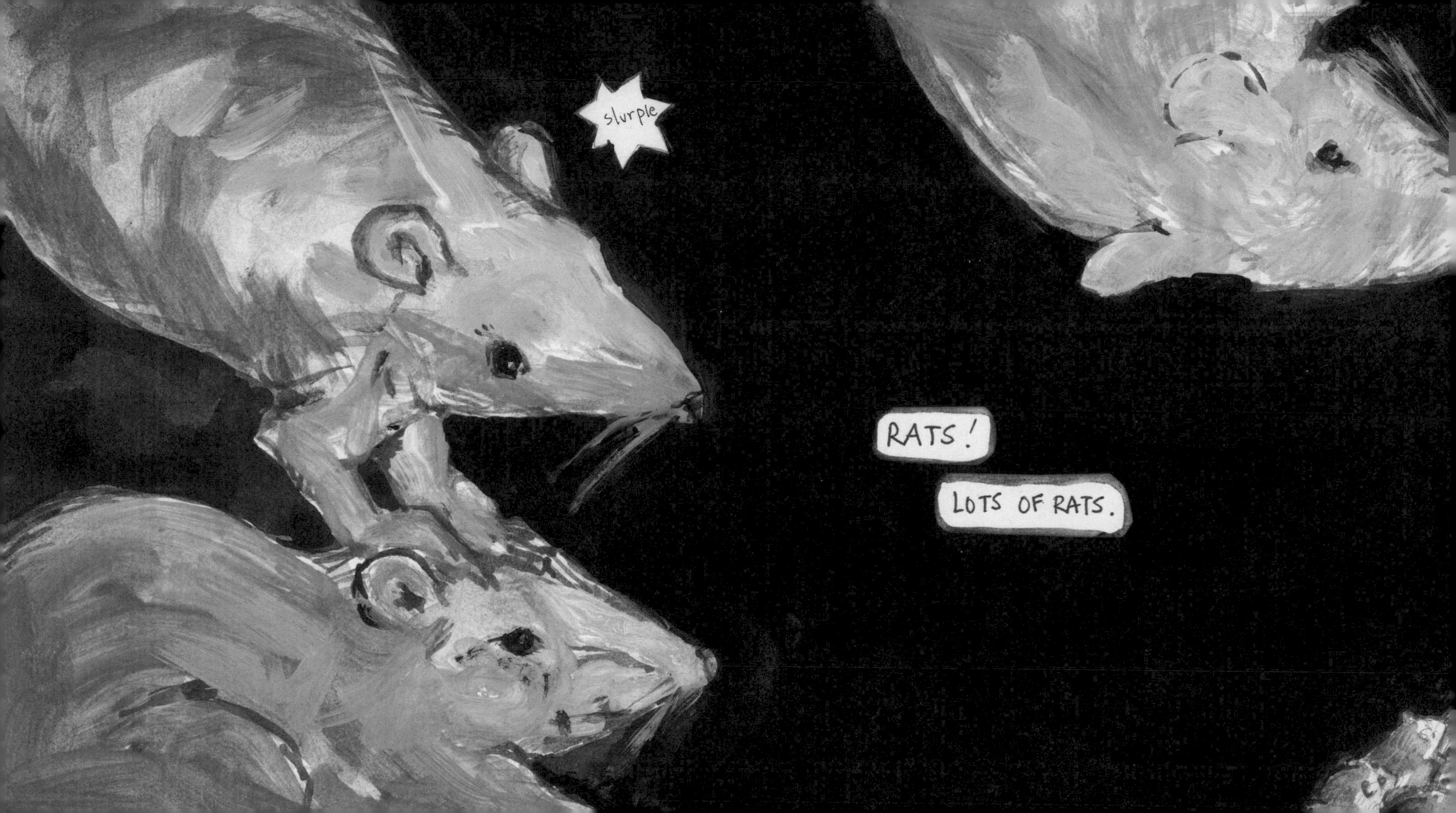
slurple
RATS!
LOTS OF RATS.

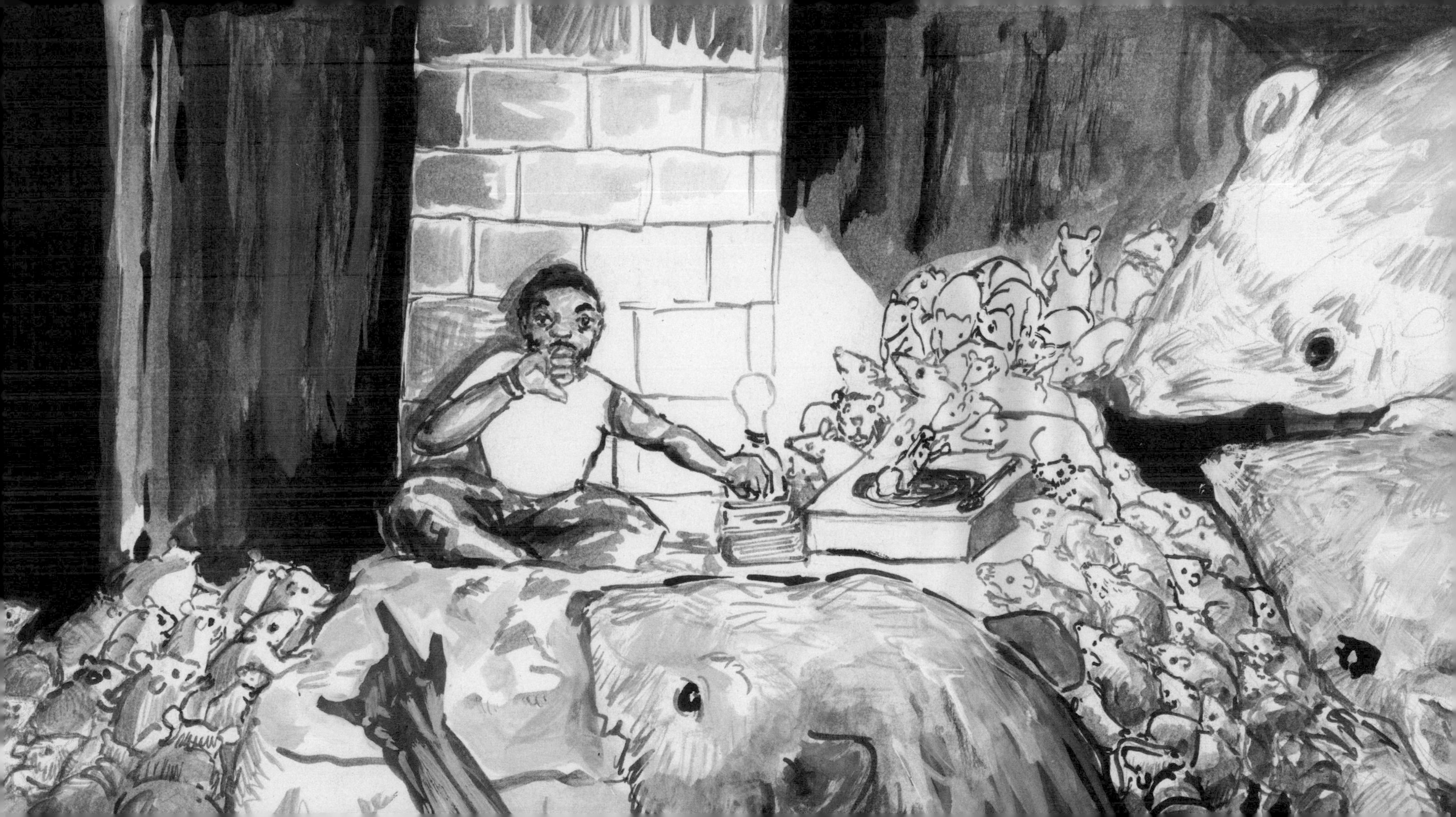

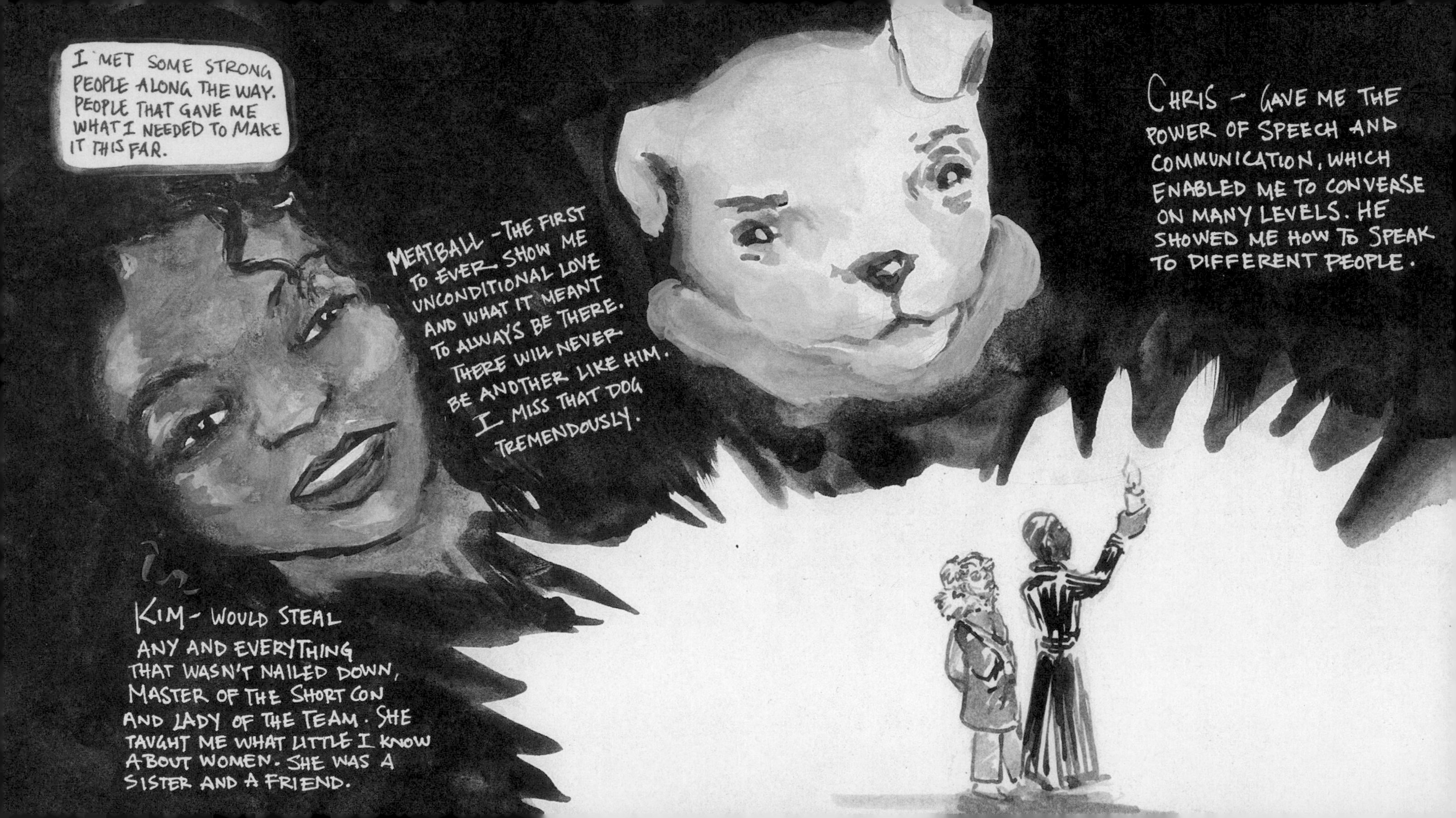
I MET SOME STRONG PEOPLE ALONG THE WAY. PEOPLE THAT GAVE ME WHAT I NEEDED TO MAKE IT THIS FAR.
MEATBALL - THE FIRST TO EVER SHOW ME UNCONDITIONAL LOVE AND WHAT IT MEANT TO ALWAYS BE THERE. THERE WILL NEVER BE ANOTHER LIKE HIM. I MISS THAT DOG TREMENDOUSLY.
CHRIS - GAVE ME THE POWER OF SPEECH AND COMMUNICATION, WHICH ENABLED ME TO CONVERSE ON MANY LEVELS. HE SHOWED ME HOW TO SPEAK TO DIFFERENT PEOPLE.
KIM - WOULD STEAL ANY AND EVERYTHING THAT WASN'T NAILED DOWN, MASTER OF THE SHORT CON AND LADY OF THE TEAM. SHE TAUGHT ME WHAT LITTLE I KNOW ABOUT WOMEN. SHE WAS A SISTER AND A FRIEND.

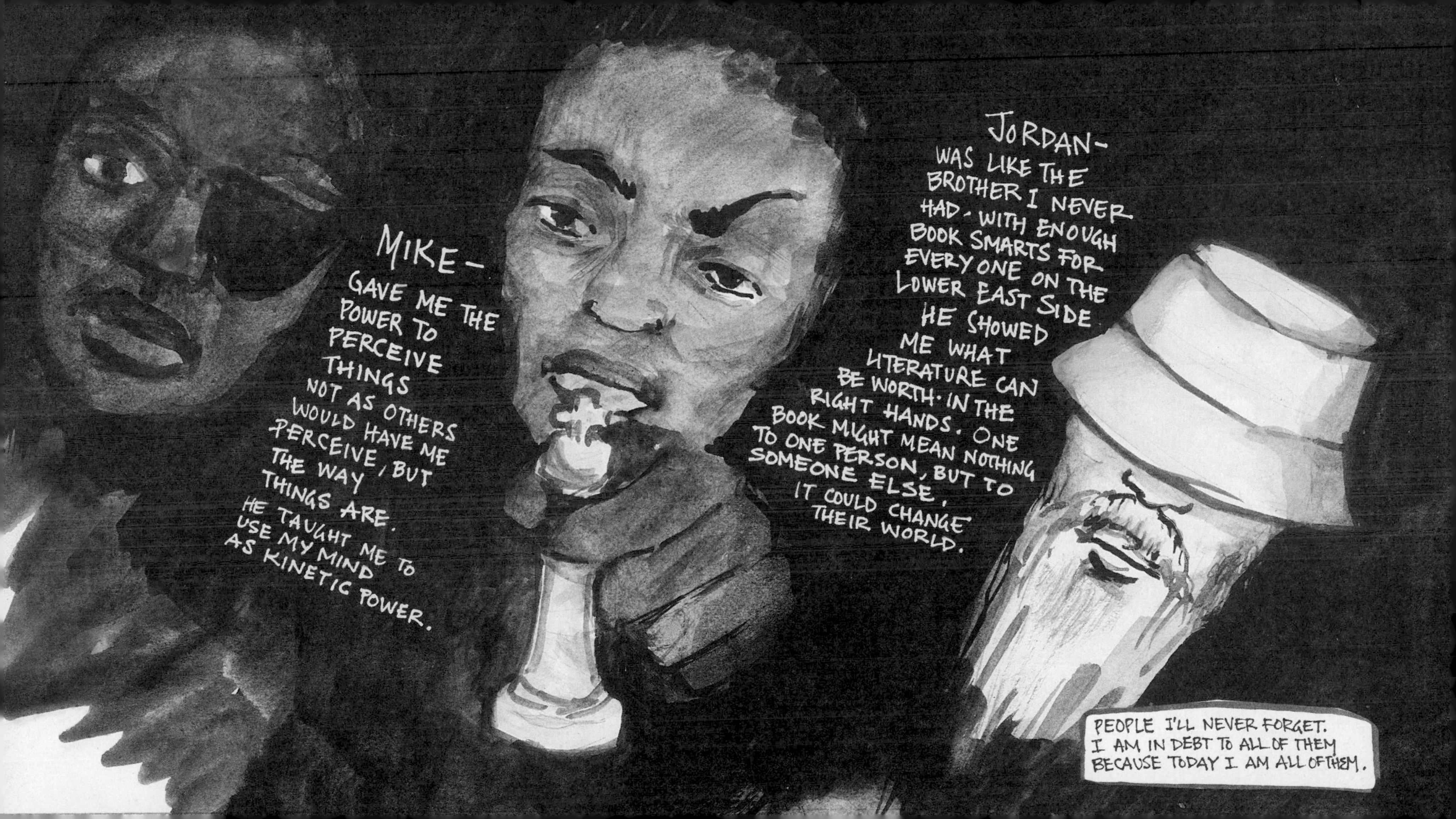
MIKE-
GAVE ME THE POWER TO PERCEIVE THINGS NOT AS OTHERS WOULD HAVE ME PERCEIVE, BUT THE WAY THINGS ARE. HE TAUGHT ME TO USE MY MIND AS KINETIC POWER.
JORDAN-
WAS LIKE THE BROTHER I NEVER HAD- WITH ENOUGH BOOK SMARTS FOR EVERYONE ON THE LOWER EAST SIDE. HE SHOWED ME WHAT LITERATURE CAN BE WORTH. IN THE RIGHT HANDS. ONE BOOK MIGHT MEAN NOTHING TO ONE PERSON, BUT TO SOMEONE ELSE, IT COULD CHANGE THEIR WORLD.
PEOPLE I'LL NEVER FORGET. I AM IN DEBT TO ALL OF THEM BECAUSE TODAY I AM ALL OF THEM.

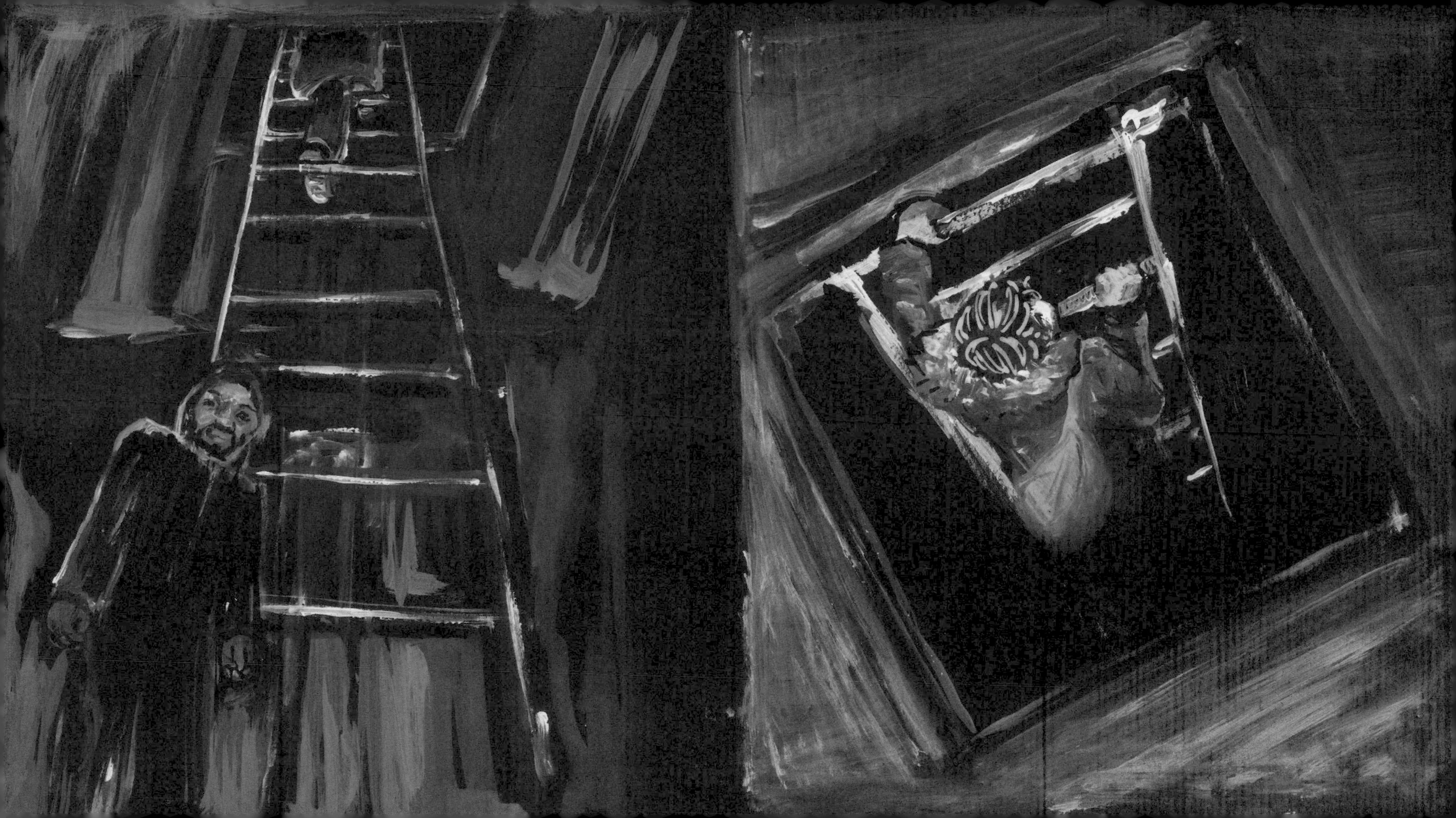

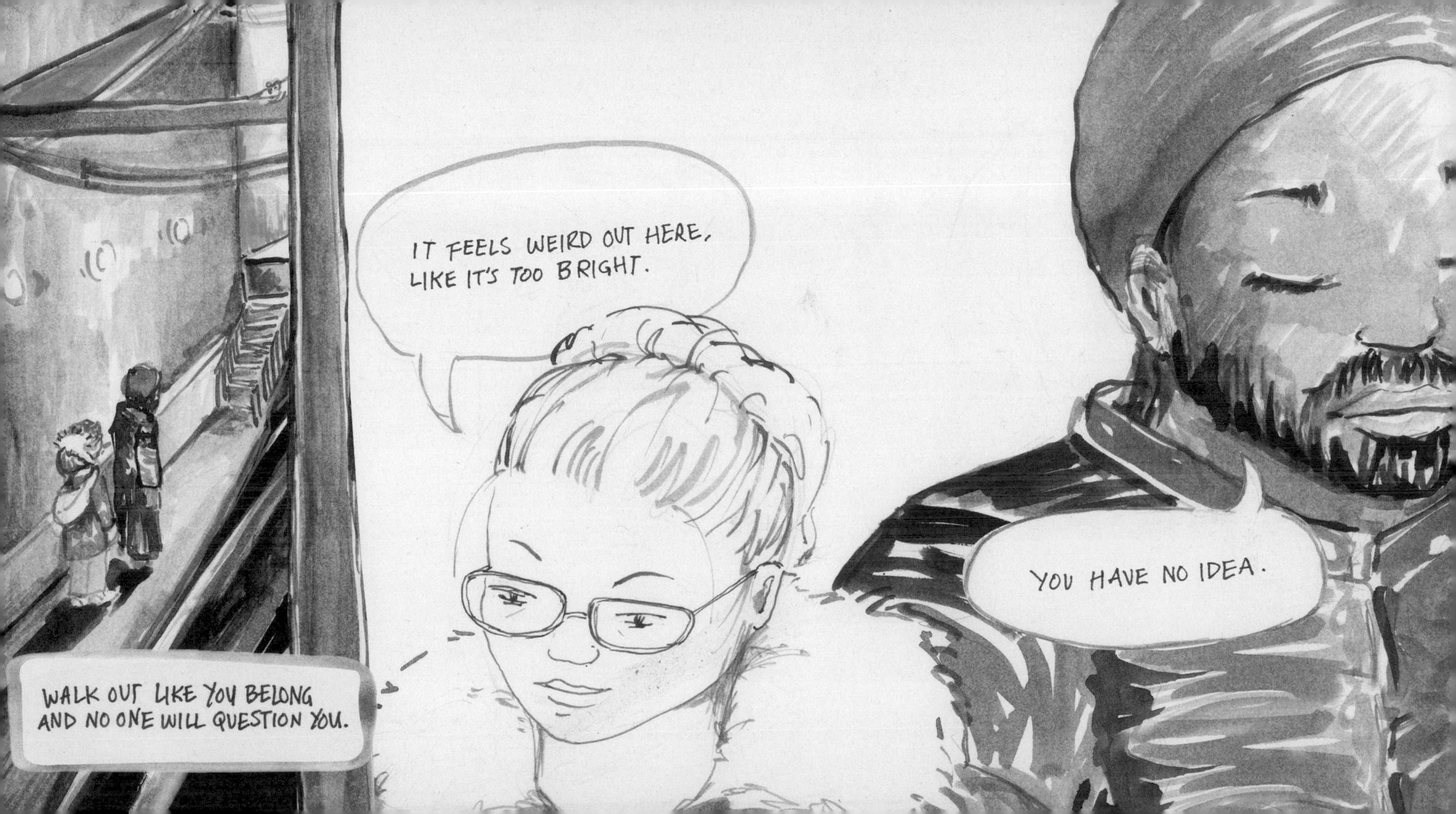
WALK OUT LIKE YOU BELONG AND NO ONE WILL QUESTION YOU.
IT FEELS WEIRD OUT HERE, LIKE IT'S TOO BRIGHT.
YOU HAVE NO IDEA.

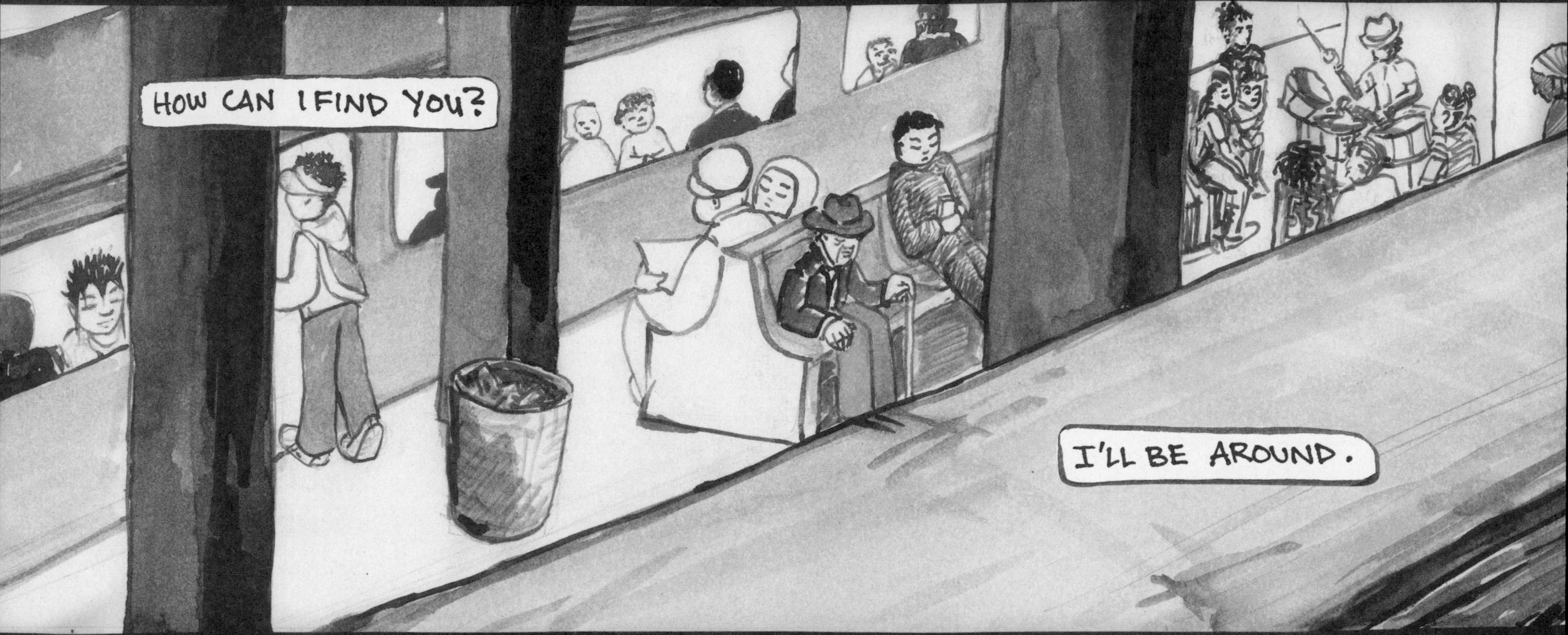
HOW CAN I FIND YOU?
I'LL BE AROUND.

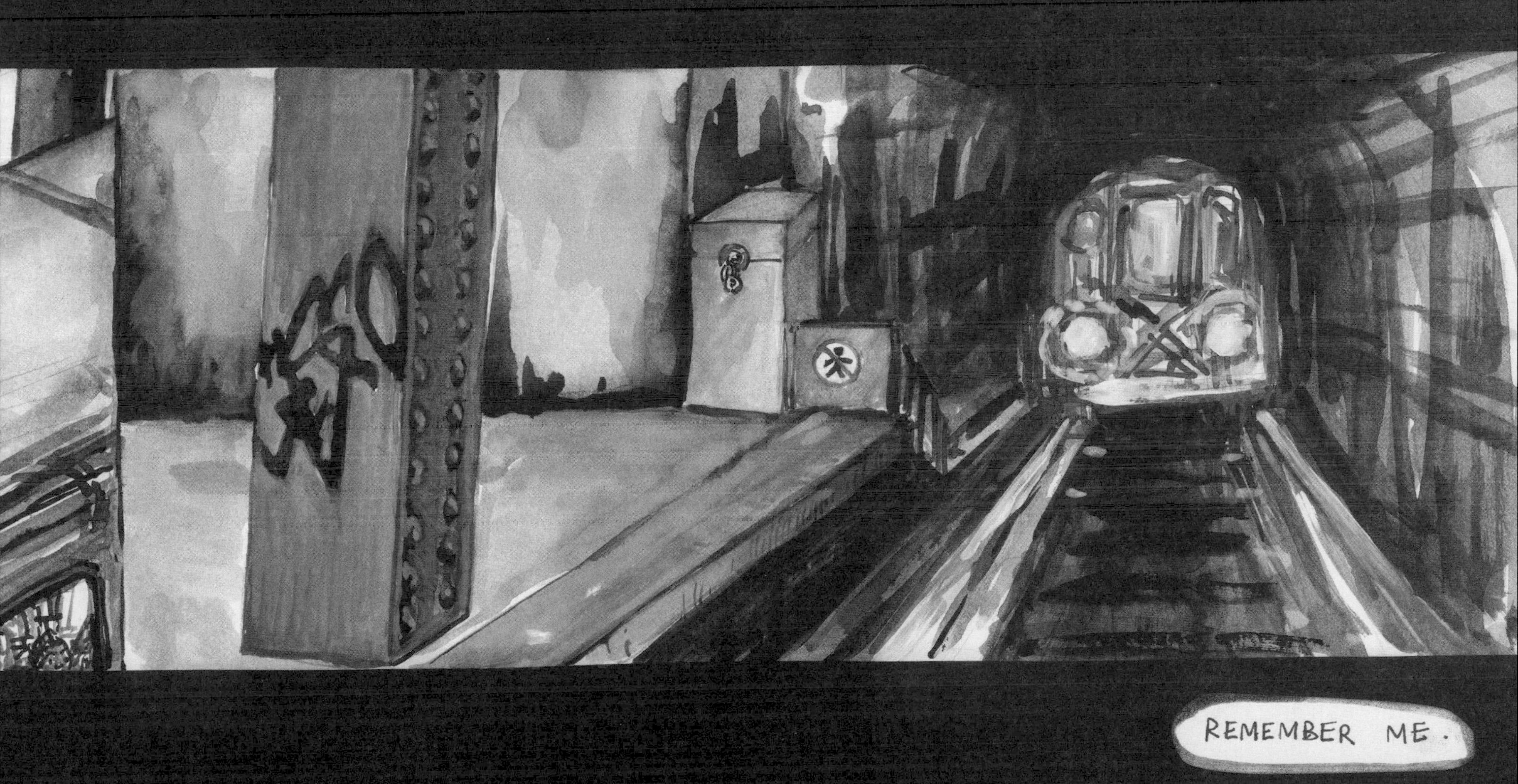
REMEMBER ME.

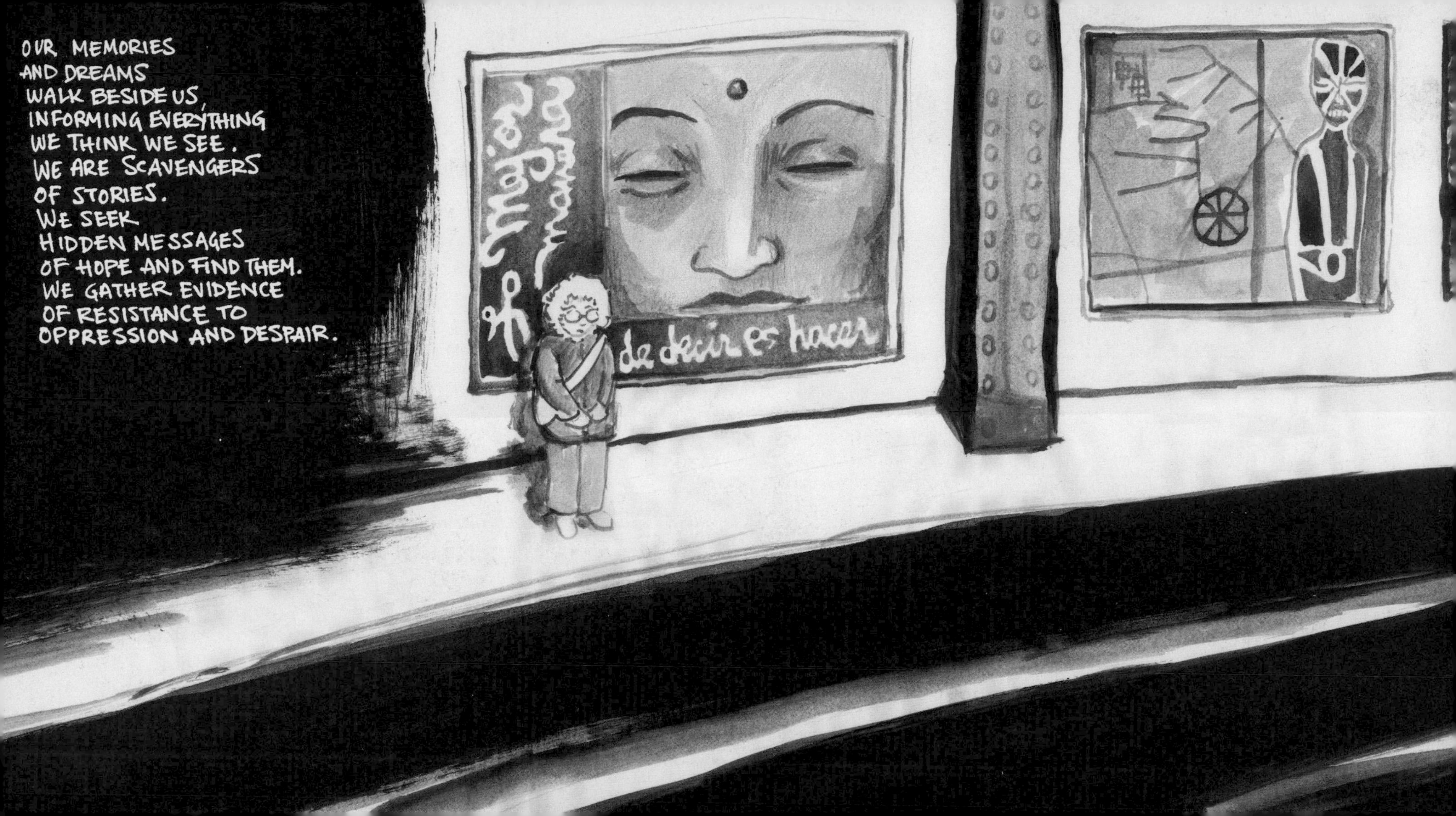
OUR MEMORIES AND DREAMS WALK BESIDE US, INFORMING EVERYTHING WE THINK WE SEE. WE ARE SCAVENGERS OF STORIES. WE SEEK HIDDEN MESSAGES OF HOPE AND FIND THEM. WE GATHER EVIDENCE OF RESISTANCE TO OPPRESSION AND DESPAIR.
mujer
de decir es hacer

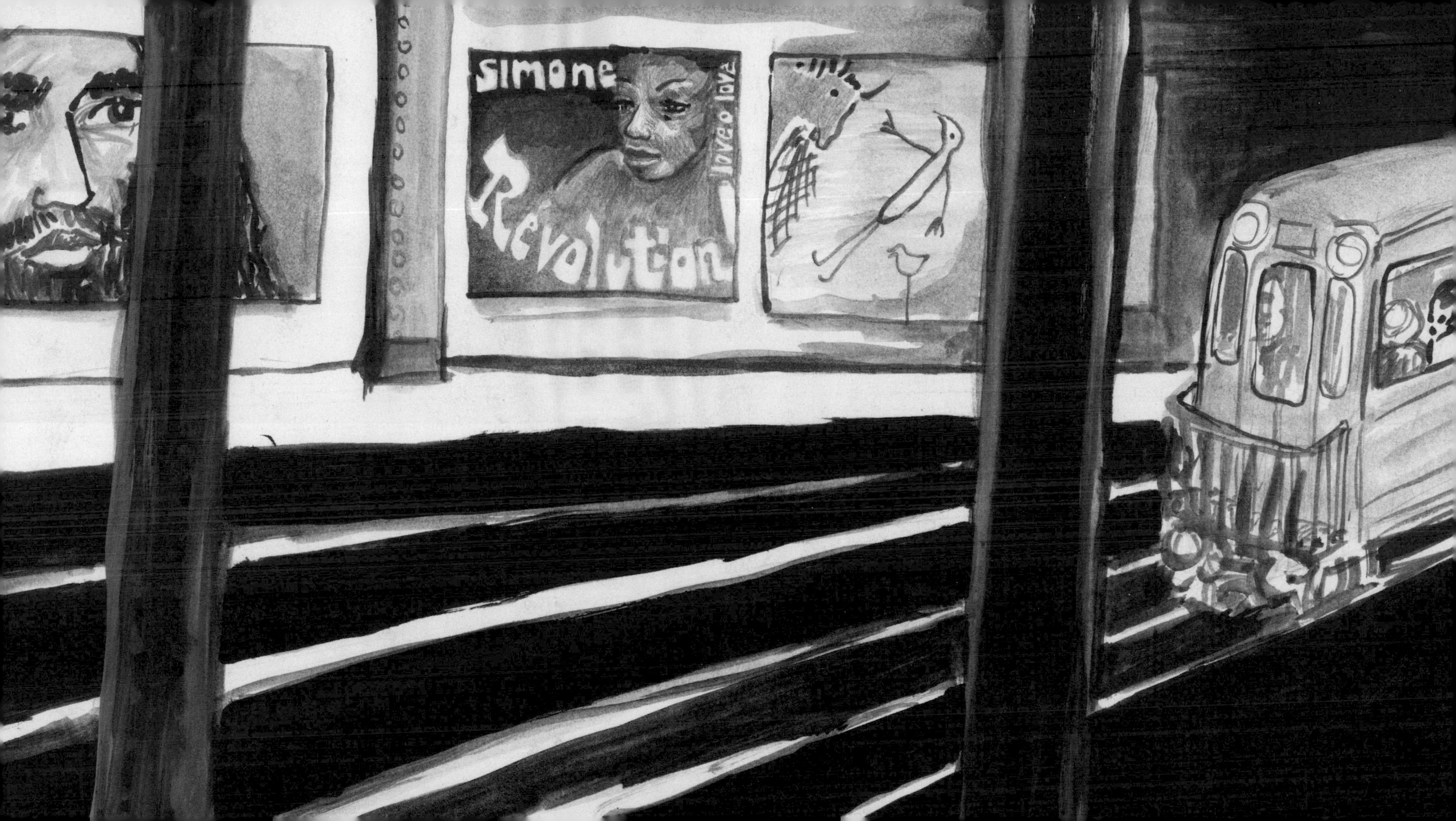
simone
Revolution
love o love

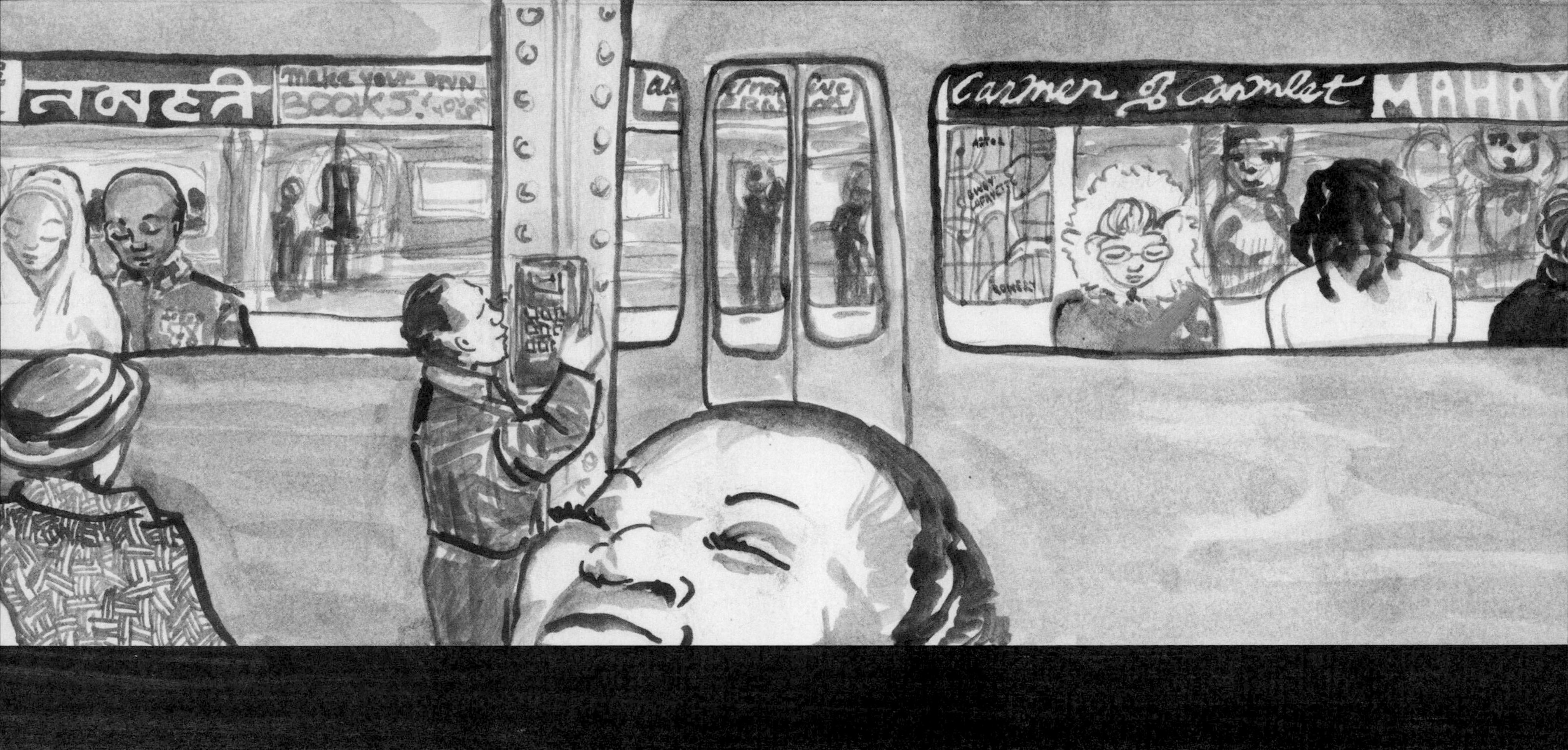
make your own
BOOKS!

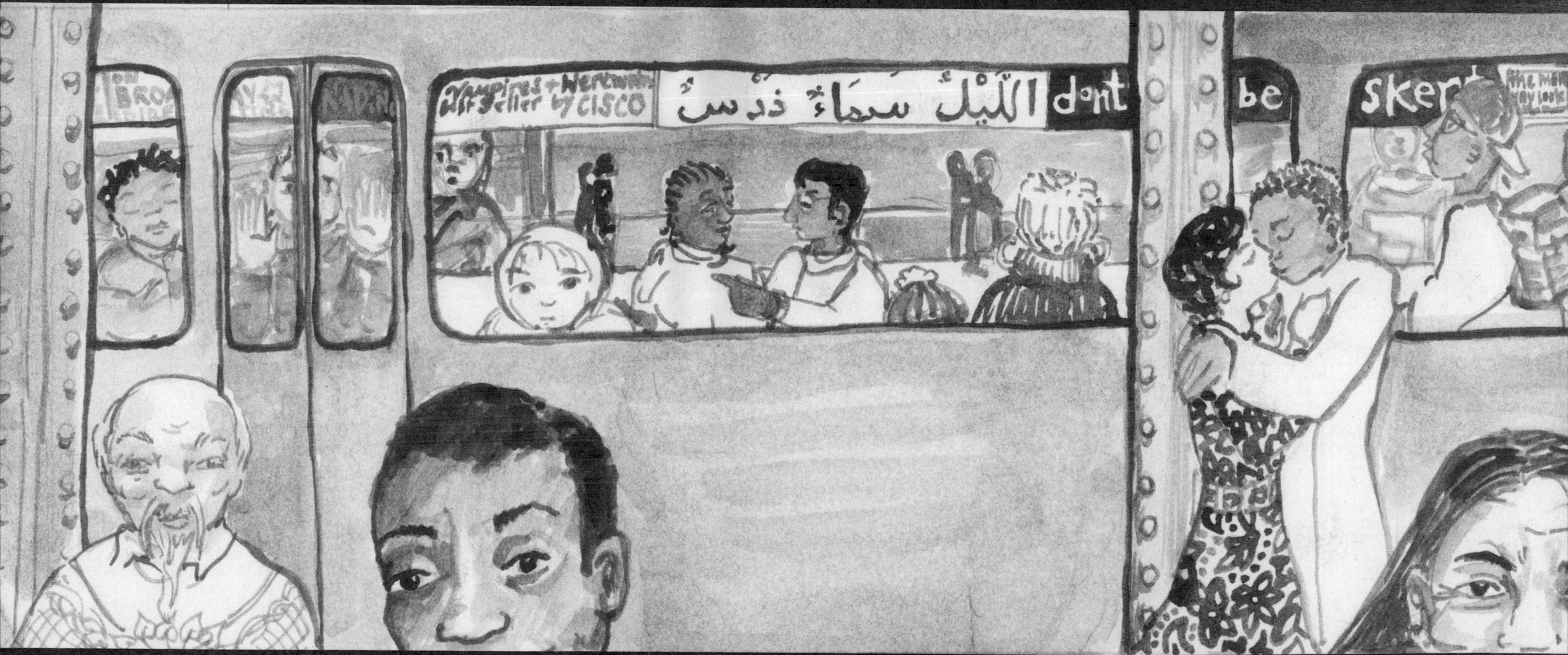

Vampires +
by CISCO
dont
be

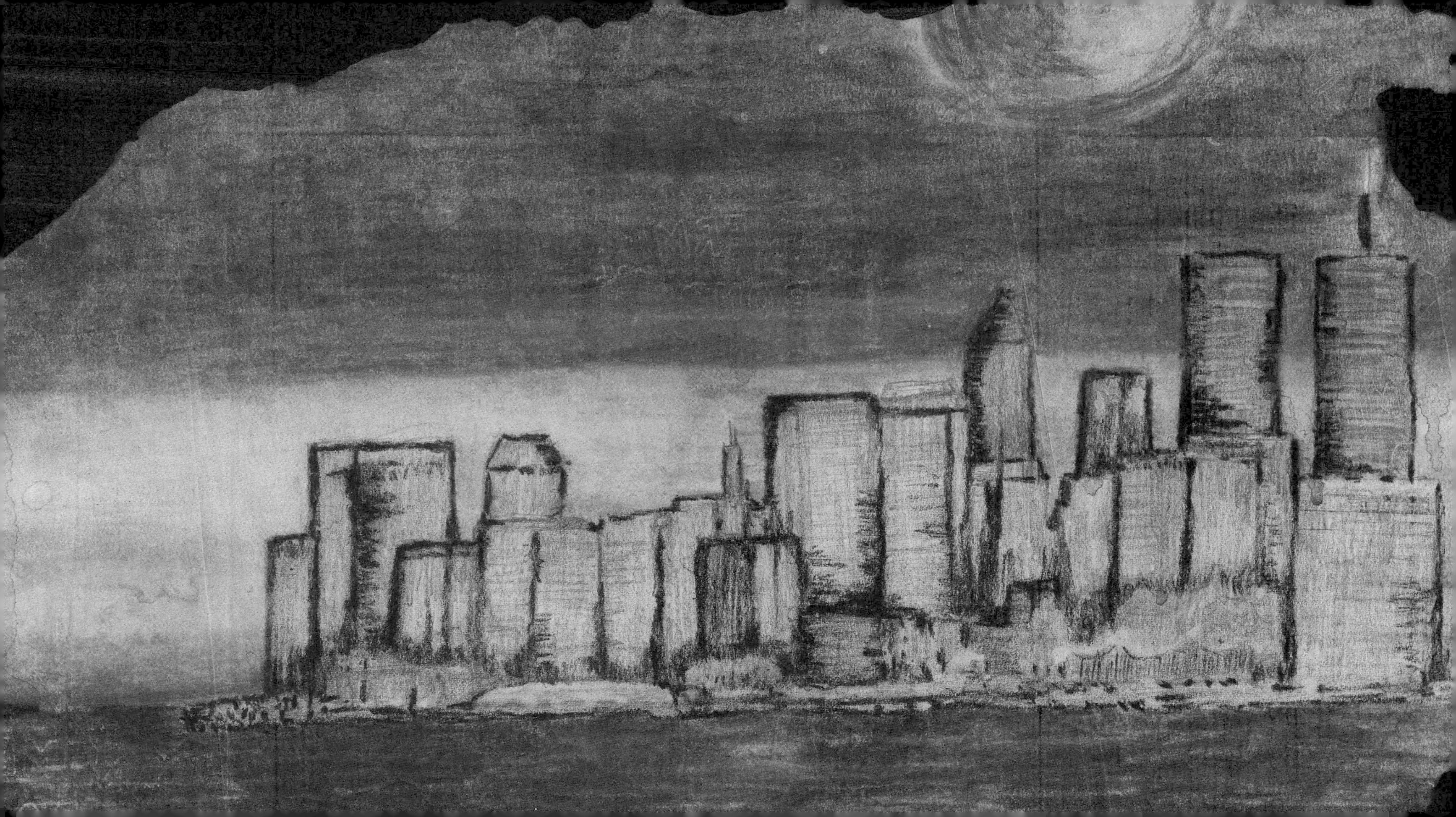

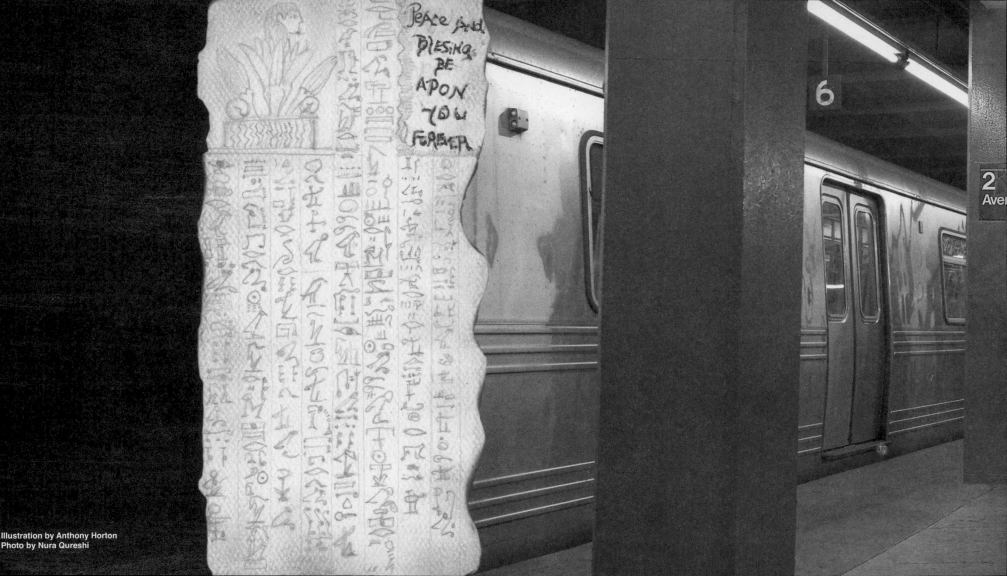

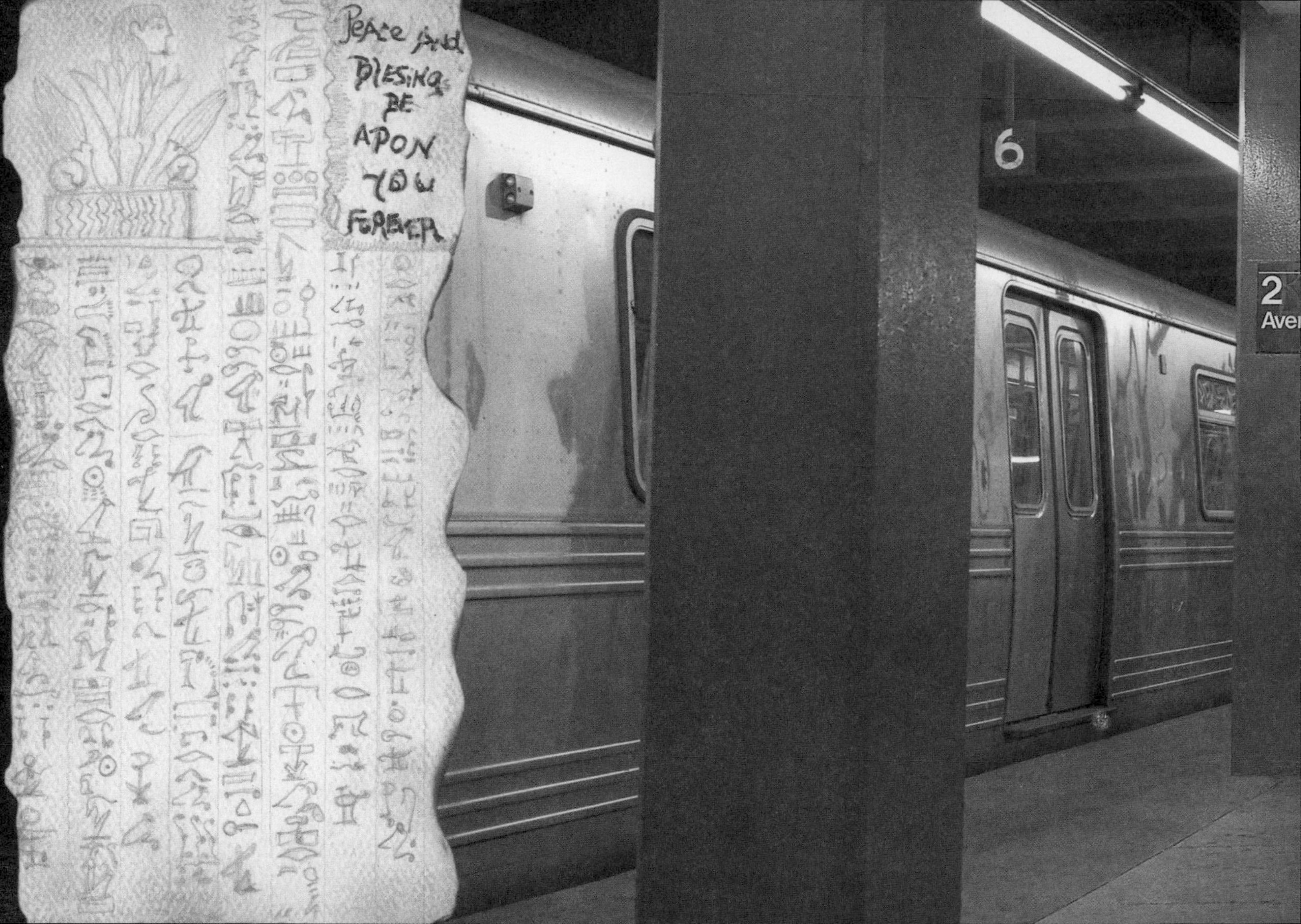
Peace And
Blesings
Be
Apon
You
Forever
6
2
Ave

Illustration by Anthony Horton
Photo by Nura Qureshi

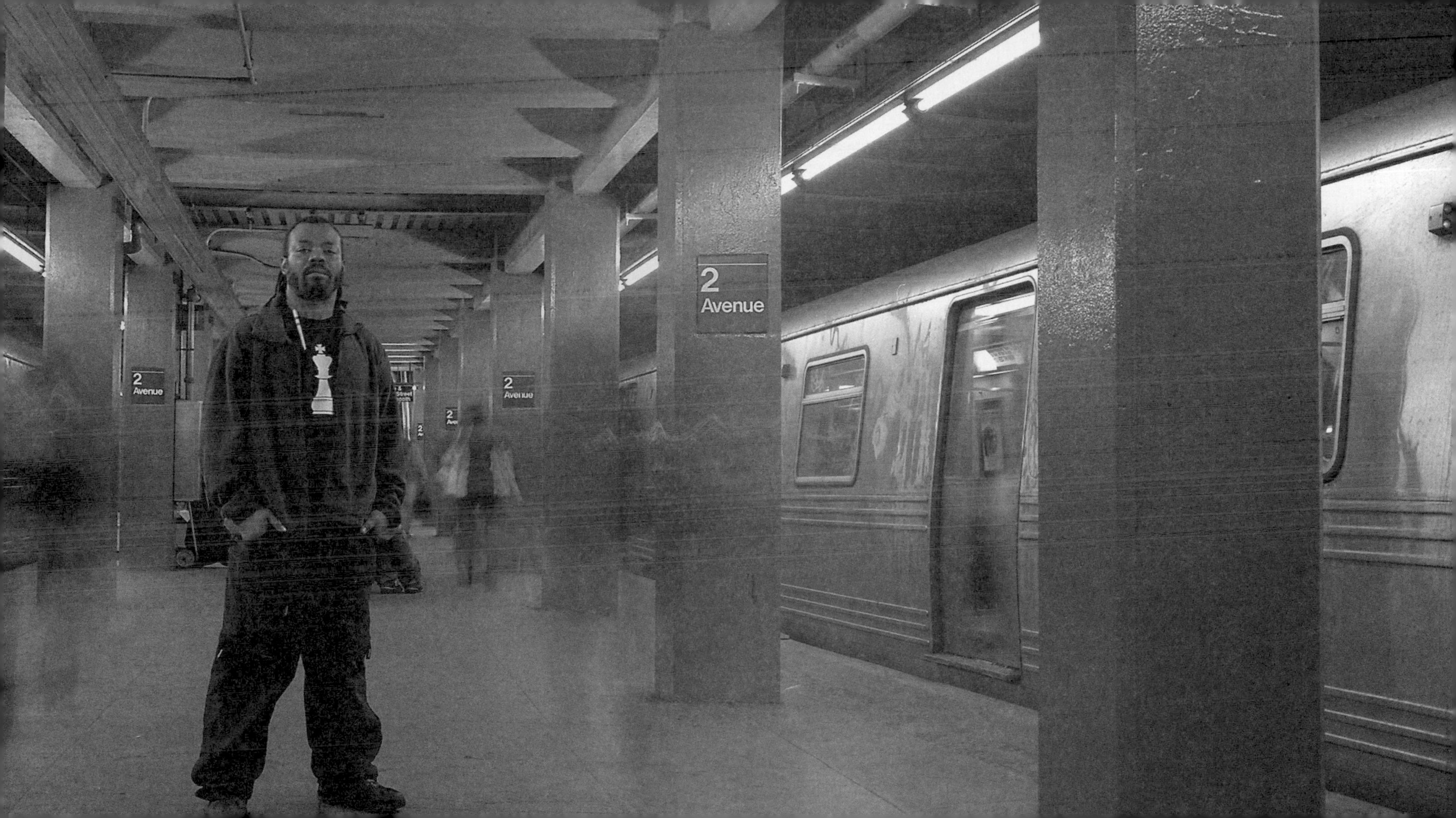
2
Avenue

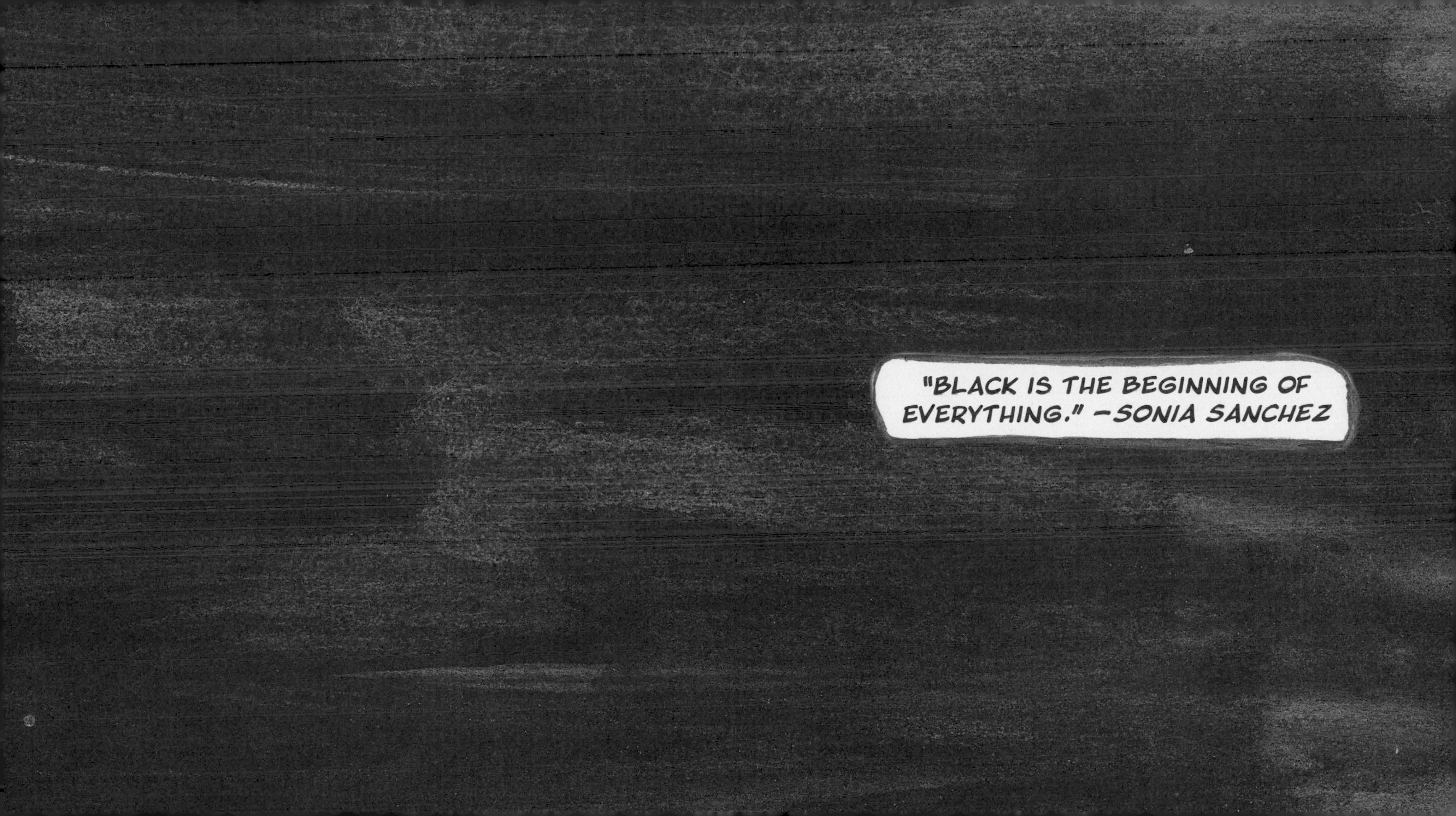
"BLACK IS THE BEGINNING OF EVERYTHING." –SONIA SANCHEZ

MY FRIEND . . .

Photo by Nura Qureshi

TONY AND I WROTE *REMEMBER ME* FOR THE ENDING OF THE BOOK BECAUSE WE BOTH WANT TO BE REMEMBERED. WE BOTH KNEW THAT SHARING STORIES—WILD AND TRUE, IMAGINED, REAL, LIVED, REALER THAN REAL AND TRUER THAN FACTS—LASTS LONGER THAN PEOPLE DO. WE WANTED CHILDREN TO KNOW THAT THEY ARE STRONG AND THEY ARE LOVED. WE ARE ALL CHILDREN.

WE BOTH HAD PEOPLE LIVING ONLY IN MEMORY WHO WE TALKED TO AND LISTENED WITH, FOR ANSWERS WE WERE NOT RECEIVING IN THE "REAL" WORLD. SO YES, SOME YEARS AFTER THIS BOOK WAS WRITTEN, TONY FOLLOWED THE PATH THAT TOOK HIM OUT OF THE PHYSICAL WORLD INTO THE SPIRIT WORLD, AND YES, I AM ANGRY AND LOST AND RIPPED IN HALF AGAIN TO LOSE A COLLABORATOR AND FRIEND WHO CHALLENGED AND CHAMPIONED ME. AND YES, I CONTINUE TO CHALLENGE AND CHAMPION ANTHONY HORTON, TONY, TONE-E, TONE OF THE WORLD.

FOR THE POSSIBLE MOVIE AND THE RE-RELEASE OF THE BOOK, I KEPT TELLING EVERYONE, "I DON'T WANT THIS BOOK/MOVIE/STORY TO END WITH TONY'S DEATH." ELISE, MY EDITOR, SAID, "TRUST YOUR READERS TO KNOW THAT DEATH IS NOT AN END."

PEOPLE OFTEN ASKED US, "BUT HOW DID YOU *REALLY* CONNECT?" I THINK WE REALLY CONNECTED AS ARTISTS, OPEN TO THE POSSIBILITY THAT THE WORLD WE SEE IS CONNECTED TO THE WORLDS WE CANNOT SEE, AND THAT GUIDANCE AND CONNECTION COMES THROUGH BEING OPEN TO THE CALL-AND-RESPONSE OF LIFE ITSELF.

I HEED HIS MESSAGES AS THEY REACH ME.

OFFICIAL REPORTS SAY THAT TONY DIED IN A FIRE IN THE TUNNELS THAT NO ONE SET. A SPARK. TONY, WHAT DO YOU WANT ME TO SAY HERE? THAT YOU DID THE PHOENIX THING? THAT YOU WENT FURTHER UNDERGROUND? YOU WERE WORKING ON YOUR NEXT BOOK, *THE OTHER SIDE*, AND *THE DARKER SUN*. YOU SHARED WITH ME THAT *PITCH BLACK* DIDN'T ADDRESS THE HARDER PARTS OF YOUR LIFE, BUT IT MADE A GOOD JUMP-OFF. *PITCH BLACK* HAS TRAVELED.

COME THROUGH, YOUNG ANCESTOR! KEEP REPRESENTING FOR THE TOUGHNESS AND THE TENDERNESS THAT ARE UNDER ATTACK YET KEEP MAKING ART AND SPEAKING TRUTH TO POWER; CRACKING JOKES THAT CUT THROUGH RACISM, SEXISM, AND HOMOPHOBIA; TELLING STORIES THAT HELP US SEE OUR FLAWED SELVES COEXISTING WITH OUR REALITY CREATING POWER. THERE IS WORK TO BE DONE HERE.

DEAR READER, YOU CALLED US BOTH TO YOU BY READING THIS BOOK. THIS STORY IS YOURS AS MUCH AS IT IS OURS. WHAT DO YOU HEAR FROM WORLDS YOU CANNOT SEE? HOW DO WE REMEMBER TOGETHER?

WITH LOVE, WHICH IS RESPECT,
YOUME

Dedicated to Love

For our grandparents

Thank you,
Dr. Milton Landowne
Dr. William H. Timberlake
Yellow Door Studio
Cannonball Press
Cisco, all the folks who stayed with us in the Tombs and those who got us out, Lisandro and Mary
Mahayana, David, Edith, Nora
Cat and Charlotte, Molly and Dom, Mali
Vin, Khan, Kyron, Shogo, Boivert
Pat Simpson, Khalil,
Groundswell and the foundations of New York City.

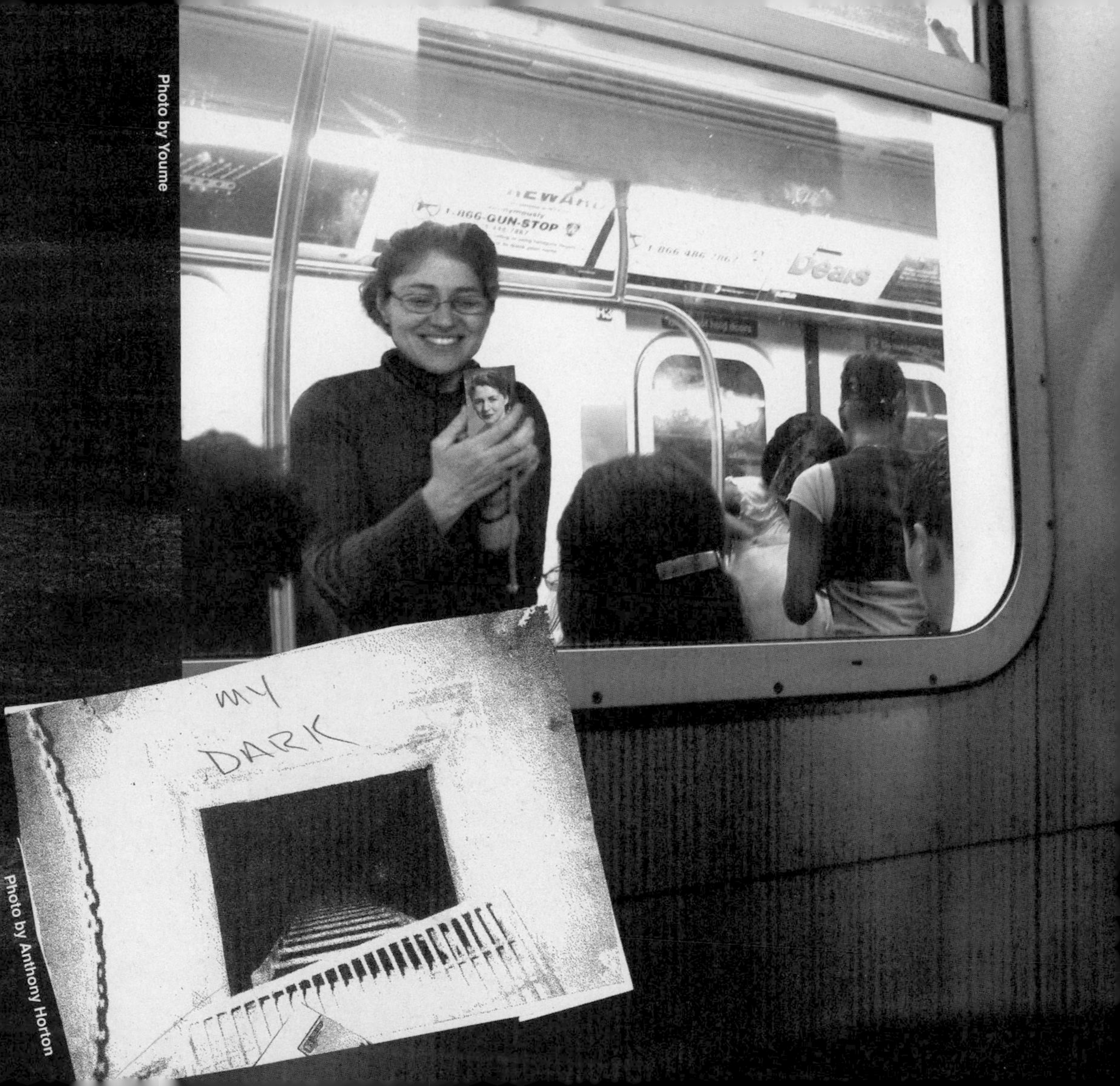
1-866-GUN-STOP
MY DARK
Photo by Youme
Photo by Anthony Horton

Cinco Puntos Press, *an imprint of* LEE & LOW BOOKS INC.,
95 Madison Avenue, New York, NY 10016, leeandlow.com

Printed in the United States.

FIRST EDITION   10 9 8 7 6 5 4 3 2 1

Cataloging in Publication data is on file with the Library of Congress.

ISBN 978-1-64379-656-7 (paperback) ISBN 978-1-93369-376-7 (e-book)

Endpapers and Cityscape by Anthony Horton

**Book design by Little Lulu's mother, Anne M. Giangiulio
For Bubba and Lucia, my light —AMG**

SUSTAINABLE FORESTRY INITIATIVE Certified Sourcing

www.forests.org
SFI-00105

Praise for
Pitch Black

Top Ten Great Graphic Novels for Teens
YALSA

Skipping Stones Honor Award
Skipping Stones Magazine

Best Children's Books of the Year
Bank Street College of Education

"I sat right down and read through [*Pitch Black*]. . . . I found it immediately engaging and also interesting in the respect that at first you think it's about homelessness then, as you read on, perhaps about race and, finally, you discover that it reaches for something beyond those thorny and somewhat shopworn subjects; the simple and pure light of hope."

—Lee Stringer, author of the award-winning book
Grand Central Winter: Stories from the Street

★ "THIS BOOK'S UNFLINCHING LOOK AT HOMELESSNESS AND THE ABILITY TO FIND HOPE AND INSPIRATION IN THE DARK WILL APPEAL GREATLY TO TEENS."
—SCHOOL LIBRARY JOURNAL, STARRED REVIEW

"[LANDOWNE AND HORTON] COLLABORATE HERE TO BRING HORTON'S STORY OF PERSEVERANCE AND HOPE TO PRINT, AND THE FLUID BLACK-AND-WHITE SEQUENTIAL PANELS TELL IT WELL. THE HORRORS ATTENDANT ON HOMELESSNESS ARE NOT SUGARCOATED, AND THE LANGUAGE IS AS RAW AND GRITTY AS ONE MIGHT EXPECT. POWERFUL."
—KIRKUS REVIEWS

"[A] SPARE BUT RICH GRAY-AND-BLACK GRAPHIC NOVEL. . . . WE WANT TO KNOW MORE ABOUT HORTON, BUT LIKE PEERING DOWN A DARK TUNNEL, WE ONLY CATCH GLIMPSES. . . . FOR ACADEMIC AND HIGH SCHOOL LIBRARIES, AND TEEN AS WELL AS ADULT COLLECTIONS IN PUBLIC LIBRARIES."
—LIBRARY JOURNAL

"THIS SHORT, COLLABORATIVE GRAPHIC NOVEL INTRODUCES TEENS TO A LIFE UNHEARD OF BY MOST. . . . THIS FULL-PAGE GRAPHIC NOVEL STYLE HELPS THE READER PERCEIVE THE DARKNESS SURROUNDING [ANTHONY] HORTON'S LIFE AND THE LIGHT THAT HIS ARTWORK GAVE HIM. THE ARTWORK DONE IN BLACK, WHITE, AND GRAY WATERCOLOR TONES IS REALISTIC AND SPARSE WITH SUBWAY DETAILS ILLUSTRATING A WIDE RANGE OF MULTICULTURAL CHARACTERS RIDING THE SUBWAY. . . . HANDSELLING OR BOOKTALKING TO READERS WHO LIKE TRUE LIFE STORIES OR GRITTY FICTION WILL FIND THIS SPECIAL TITLE AND FORMAT AN AUDIENCE."
—VOYA MAGAZINE